INTRODUCING
ISSUES WITH
OPPOSING
VIEWPOINTS®

WITHDRAWN

Disabilities
Affecting
Learning

Mike Wilson, *Book Editor*

GREENHAVEN PRESS
A part of Gale, Cengage Learning

GALE
CENGAGE Learning

Detroit • New York • San Francisco • New Haven, Conn • Waterville, Maine • London

Christine Nasso, *Publisher*
Elizabeth Des Chenes, *Managing Editor*

Articles in Greenhaven Press anthologies are often edited for length to meet page requirements. In addition, original titles of these works are changed to clearly present the main thesis and to explicitly indicate the author's opinion. Every effort is made to ensure that Greenhaven Press accurately reflects the original intent of the authors. Every effort has been made to trace the owners of copyrighted material.

Cover image copyright © Leah-Anne Thompson, 2009. Used under license from Shutterstock.com

LIBRARY OF CONGRESS CATALOGING-IN-PUBLICATION DATA

Disabilities affecting learning / Mike Wilson, book editor.
    p. cm. -- (Introducing issues with opposing viewpoints)
 Includes bibliographical references and index.
 ISBN 978-0-7377-4338-8 (hardcover)
 1. Learning disabled children. 2. Autistic children. 3. Dyslexic children. 4. Attention-deficit disordered children. I. Wilson, Mike, 1954-
  LC4704.D565 2009
  371.94--dc22

2009013593

Printed in the United States of America
1 2 3 4 5 6 7 13 12 11 10 09

Contents

Foreword   5

Introduction   7

Chapter 1: Are Disabilities Affecting Learning a Serious Problem?

1. Dyslexia Is a Serious Problem   11
   E. Ruth Wesby

2. Dyslexia Is Widely Misunderstood   17
   David Mills

3. Attention Deficit Hyperactivity Disorder Is a
   Serious Problem   23
   PR Newswire Contributor

4. Attention Deficit Hyperactivity Disorder Is a Myth   29
   Fred A. Baughman Jr. and Craig Hovey

5. Autism Is a Serious Problem   38
   Chris Emery

6. Many Factors Have Contributed to the Rise in
   Autism Diagnoses   44
   Mike Stobbe

7. Autism Disabilities Vary Greatly   51
   Robert Nohle

Chapter 2: What Harm Is Caused by Disabilities Affecting Learning?

1. Learning Disabilities Cause Behavioral Problems   57
   Diana Mahoney

2. Children with Learning Disabilities Are Vulnerable to Abuse   64
   Freda Briggs

3. Autism Is Linked to Changes in the Brain   71
   National Institutes of Health

4. ADHD Negatively Affects Adults in Numerous Ways   76
   Steve Bates

5. ADHD Prevents Children from Making Friends   81
   Ascribe Higher Education News Service

Chapter 3: How Should Society Address Disabilities Affecting Learning?

1. Special Education Can Help Students with
   Learning Disabilities   87
   John W. Porter

2. Special Education Is Too Costly   93
   Jennifer Mann

3. ADHD Drugs Can Help Many Children   100
   Darshak Sanghavi

4. ADHD Drugs Are Overprescribed and Harmful
   to Children   106
   Barbara Davies

5. Preventing Exposure to Toxins Could Reduce
   Learning Disabilities   115
   Steven Kouris

6. Schools Should Prepare Learning-Disabled Students
   for Employment   121
   D. Richard Johnson, Daryl F. Mellard, and Paula Lancaster

Facts About Disabilities Affecting Learning   126
Organizations to Contact   129
For Further Reading   134
Index   139
Picture Credits   144

Foreword

Indulging in a wide spectrum of ideas, beliefs, and perspectives is a critical cornerstone of democracy. After all, it is often debates over differences of opinion, such as whether to legalize abortion, how to treat prisoners, or when to enact the death penalty, that shape our society and drive it forward. Such diversity of thought is frequently regarded as the hallmark of a healthy and civilized culture. As the Reverend Clifford Schutjer of the First Congregational Church in Mansfield, Ohio, declared in a 2001 sermon, "Surrounding oneself with only like-minded people, restricting what we listen to or read only to what we find agreeable is irresponsible. Refusing to entertain doubts once we make up our minds is a subtle but deadly form of arrogance." With this advice in mind, Introducing Issues with Opposing Viewpoints books aim to open readers' minds to the critically divergent views that comprise our world's most important debates.

Introducing Issues with Opposing Viewpoints simplifies for students the enormous and often overwhelming mass of material now available via print and electronic media. Collected in every volume is an array of opinions that captures the essence of a particular controversy or topic. Introducing Issues with Opposing Viewpoints books embody the spirit of nineteenth-century journalist Charles A. Dana's axiom: "Fight for your opinions, but do not believe that they contain the whole truth, or the only truth." Absorbing such contrasting opinions teaches students to analyze the strength of an argument and compare it to its opposition. From this process readers can inform and strengthen their own opinions, or be exposed to new information that will change their minds. Introducing Issues with Opposing Viewpoints is a mosaic of different voices. The authors are statesmen, pundits, academics, journalists, corporations, and ordinary people who have felt compelled to share their experiences and ideas in a public forum. Their words have been collected from newspapers, journals, books, speeches, interviews, and the Internet, the fastest growing body of opinionated material in the world.

Introducing Issues with Opposing Viewpoints shares many of the well-known features of its critically acclaimed parent series, Opposing Viewpoints. The articles are presented in a pro/con format, allowing readers to absorb divergent perspectives side by side. Active reading questions preface each viewpoint, requiring the student to approach the material thoughtfully and carefully. Useful charts, graphs, and cartoons supplement each article. A thorough introduction provides readers with crucial background on an issue. An annotated bibliography points the reader toward articles, books, and Web sites that contain additional information on the topic. An appendix of organizations to contact contains a wide variety of charities, nonprofit organizations, political groups, and private enterprises that each hold a position on the issue at hand. Finally, a comprehensive index allows readers to locate content quickly and efficiently.

Introducing Issues with Opposing Viewpoints is also significantly different from Opposing Viewpoints. As the series title implies, its presentation will help introduce students to the concept of opposing viewpoints and learn to use this material to aid in critical writing and debate. The series' four-color, accessible format makes the books attractive and inviting to readers of all levels. In addition, each viewpoint has been carefully edited to maximize a reader's understanding of the content. Short but thorough viewpoints capture the essence of an argument. A substantial, thought-provoking essay question placed at the end of each viewpoint asks the student to further investigate the issues raised in the viewpoint, compare and contrast two authors' arguments, or consider how one might go about forming an opinion on the topic at hand. Each viewpoint contains sidebars that include at-a-glance information and handy statistics. A Facts About section located in the back of the book further supplies students with relevant facts and figures.

Following in the tradition of the Opposing Viewpoints series, Greenhaven Press continues to provide readers with invaluable exposure to the controversial issues that shape our world. As John Stuart Mill once wrote: "The only way in which a human being can make some approach to knowing the whole of a subject is by hearing what can be said about it by persons of every variety of opinion and studying all modes in which it can be looked at by every character of mind. No wise man ever acquired his wisdom in any mode but this." It is to this principle that Introducing Issues with Opposing Viewpoints books are dedicated.

Introduction

"In my reading group each time I attempted to unscramble the words that floated around in my head, I tried to tell Mrs. C. to let me stop. I couldn't breathe. I felt trapped. I was trying so hard and desperately wanted to be like everyone else. I learned that year to hide in the bathroom to escape reading out loud. I would stare at the mirror, hoping to God that no one would walk in on me crying."

—Jonathan Mooney, *Learning Outside the Lines: Two Ivy League Students with Learning Disabilities and ADHD Give You the Tools*, 2000

The quote above illustrates the isolation experienced by those who have learning disabilities. However, during the past two hundred years, medicine and the social sciences have made progress toward reducing such isolation through discoveries about the process of learning, potential causes of learning disabilities, and methods to improve learning skills.

In 1802 Franz J. Gall, Napoleon's surgeon, recognized a connection between brain injuries in soldiers and expressive language disorders. This discovery, later proven more substantially, that certain parts of the brain control certain emotions and actions was a revolutionary idea at the time. During the next two centuries, and continuing today, scientists have gained more precise knowledge about how the brain processes experience and information, data relevant to identifying brain parts and the processes that are critical to learning.

From various quarters the notion of learning disabilities as a specific type of condition began to appear. In 1867 German teacher Heinrich Stotzner founded a school for children who were slow learners. Stotzner did not consider the children retarded; rather he viewed them as handicapped by weak memory and poor motor coordination, and he treated them with remedial, or corrective, teaching.

German physician Adolph Kussmaul is credited with being the first person to identify dyslexia, which he called "word blindness." Though the term "dyslexia" was coined by Rudolf Berlin in 1887, the term "word blindness" continued in use for some time, famously in the work of Scottish physician James Hinshelwood during the early 1900s. Hinshelwood theorized that "word blindness" was caused by damage to the brain and was probably hereditary. Today, dyslexia is regarded as a neurobiological condition that often is hereditary and genetic in origin.

Samuel Orton, an American physician, studied reading difficulties in children during the early 1900s. He hypothesized that these children had failed to establish the cerebral organization necessary to associate visual words with their spoken forms. Orton also observed that the children tended to reverse letters and be ambidextrous—having equal ability in both hands—or have mixed-handedness, which involves using one hand for some tasks and the other hand for other tasks. This observation led him to hypothesize that left and right brain functions were not properly integrated. Orton developed the concept of "multisensory" teaching that integrated kinesthetic (movement-based) and tactile (based on touch and other senses) learning strategies with the teaching of visual and auditory concepts. Along the same lines, psychiatrist Grace Fernard's kinesthetic approach involved tracing words while saying the names and sounds of the letters. Orton and psychologist Anna Gillingham developed the "Orton-Gillingham" teaching method, which teaches in a systematic and multisensory way the sound structure of language. This method is still the basis of the most prevalent forms of teaching intended to correct dyslexia.

Another disability that affects learning is attention deficit hyperactivity disorder (ADHD). The first clinical description of ADHD was reported in 1902 by British physician George Still. He noticed that some of his young patients were impulsive and hyperactive, had limited attention spans, and suffered from mood swings. It was theorized that the behavior was caused by minimal brain damage, later modified to minimal brain dysfunction (MBD) as the condition appeared to exist without known brain damage. Hyperactive Child Syndrome also was a term used to refer to the condition. During the 1970s, the work of Canadian researcher Virginia Douglas suggested attention deficit, rather than hyperactivity, was of greater significance in the syndrome. The 1980 edition of the *Diagnostic and Statistical Manual* (*DSM III*) defined and named the disorder ADD. However, in 1987, *DSM III* replaced ADD with ADHD, the term used today, and divided it into three types: Predominantly Inattentive Type, Predominantly Hyperactive-Impulsive Type, and Combined Type (having symptoms of both types).

Much controversy has developed over the very diagnosis of ADHD. Critics have complained that the criteria for diagnosing ADHD are so vague that many children with persistent unwanted behaviors may be classified as having ADHD. This skepticism is increased by uncertainty regarding the cause of ADHD. ADHD tends to run in families, indicating a genetic component. Some evidence indicates that differences exist between the brains of persons with ADHD and those without the condition. Also, controversy exists over how to treat ADHD. Options include medications, behavior-changing therapies, and educational interventions.

Like ADHD, autism has attracted tremendous media attention and has sparked controversy over issues like diagnosis and treatment. The word "autism" was coined by Swiss psychiatrist Eugen Bleuler in 1908 to refer to schizophrenic patients who appeared disconnected and self-absorbed. In 1943 the American child psychiatrist Leo Kanner described as autistic children demonstrating what he termed "autistic aloneness" and "insistence on sameness," characteristics still regarded as typical of the range of disorders now known as autism spectrum disorders (ASD). In 1944 Austrian physician Hans Asperger (later to have an ASD named after him) described affected children as autistic psychopaths.

Starting in the late 1960s, autism was established as a separate syndrome, distinguished from mental retardation and schizophrenia and from other developmental disorders. Research also demonstrated that there were benefits to involving parents of autistic children in active programs of therapy. By the 1980s, many researchers were convinced that ASD grows out of neurological disturbances. Research also made clear that autistic children ranged from severely disabled to highly intelligent but eccentric. The Autism Society of America has stated that "just as there is no one symptom or behavior that identifies individuals with ASD, there is no single treatment that will be effective for all people on the spectrum." To varying degrees, however, individuals can learn to function and even thrive within the confines of ASD.

The articles in *Introducing Issues with Opposing Viewpoints: Disabilities Affecting Learning* reflect disagreement about the extent, cause, and treatment of various disabilities that have an impact on learning. However, most can agree that the isolation experienced by those with these disabilities can be acute. Medicine and social sciences have made great strides in reducing that isolation, though most experts acknowledge that much more can still be accomplished.

Chapter 1

Are Disabilities Affecting Learning a Serious Problem?

How best to diagnose and treat learning disabilities that include dyslexia and autism has been the subject of much discussion in the last thirty years.

Dyslexia Is a Serious Problem

E. Ruth Wesby

"Difficulties such as dyslexia affect 20 percent of the U.S. population— or one in five."

E. Ruth Wesby argues in this viewpoint that many dyslexic students are not evaluated or given the proper programs they need to learn to read. Undiagnosed dyslexia, she argues, affects learning throughout a child's educational career, because reading is the foundation of effective learning. Early detection and intervention, she says, is crucial in addressing the serious problem of dyslexia. Wesby is a former teacher in Cleveland, Ohio.

AS YOU READ, CONSIDER THE FOLLOWING QUESTIONS:
1. According to the author, what type of deficit causes dyslexia?
2. What is the intelligence level of children with dyslexia, according to Wesby?
3. How is poor reading related to school suspensions and expulsions, in Wesby's view?

E. Ruth Wesby, "Dyslexia: Serious Reading Problem Goes Undiagnosed, Victims Neglected," *Call and Post* (Cleveland), vol. 89, February 10, 2005, p. 2B. Copyright © 2005 by King Media Enterprises, Inc. Reproduced by permission.

R eading is the heart of the educational system in our nation's schools. Much time, effort and expertise are given to reading, yet, far too many children are not learning to read.

Can it be that we have forgotten the varied pathways learners take in being taught to read? Can it be we have failed to identify the students who take the path "less traveled" in learning to read? When thoughts of the dyslexic learners come to mind, the answer can very well be a resounding "yes."

Dyslexic Students Are Not Served

In our nation's schools, the curriculum is geared to those who handle the language, both oral and written expression, in the normal manner with ease. For the readers discovering that words are challenging and hard work, and for those who require a different course in expressing the language, there is neglect.

The dyslexic reader is the student whose path to learning how to read is different. Dyslexia, a language-based learning disability, remains undiagnosed and unaddressed.

But, success starts with reading! When children become good readers in their early years, they are more likely to become better learners throughout their school years and beyond. Studies from Yale University indicate that difficulties such as dyslexia affect 20 percent of the U.S. population—or one in five.

FAST FACT

As many as 15 percent of American students may be dyslexic.

In busy classrooms where there are children with dyslexia, traditional programs are not always effective for the dyslexic student, particularly where there is no evaluation. Students with dyslexia need special programs to learn to read, to write, to speak and to spell.

Certain behaviors are missed when instructors do not recognize dyslexia.

Phonological Deficit

The dyslexic child is one who has a phonological deficit. The child does not hear the letter sounds. Hearing the sounds of letters is a

Dyslexic children have difficulty hearing letter sounds and require special instruction in phonetics from speech therapists.

must. The letter sound system is critical in reading. The reader must convert the letters into sounds, or phonetics, and decode. These are two major components of reading. The dyslexic reader requires specialized instruction in order to overcome the deficit.

Dyslexia describes a different kind of mind, often gifted and productive. The gap exists between aptitude and achievement in schools. Dyslexic readers have normal to high intelligence. Contrary to beliefs, dyslexic readers are not "lazy, stupid or dumb." They do not read "backwards."

Dyslexia has no boundaries. It occurs among all groups, regardless of age, race, gender or income.

Detection and Early Intervention

Educators must respect research. Although dyslexia is genetically influenced, having dyslexia does not spell biological failure. Early detection and intervention must take place. Symptoms must be noted and acted upon.

Congress has criticized the Special Education Sector for not replicating research practices. Placing dyslexic children in special needs classes without certified teachers who are trained in the specialized instructional methodology certainly compounds the reading problems. Language deficiency is the root of most learning disabilities.

In communication with educational leadership and legislators in our state of Ohio, persons to whom we entrust the education of our children, the writer has found to date no plan or action for meeting the needs of the dyslexic child. The reading problem continues to remain invisible, therefore, undiagnosed and unaddressed.

Instructors of reading can be trained and certified through staff development. Curriculum material on dyslexia should be a part of Media resource centers in the schools. Information is vital for educators to become informed of the reading disorder.

The approach to language acquisition requires a multi-sensory structure, or a systematic approach in language instruction. Instruction which is multi-sensory employs all pathways of learning at the same time—seeing, hearing, touching, writing and speaking. The method is a way of teaching the code of the written language in a direct and explicit manner. Bit by bit the code is taught sequentially and the focus is on teaching the rules of the written language, so that conversion of the letters into sounds or phonemes can be acquired by the child with dyslexia.

Poor Reading Can Lead to Behavior Problems

The poor reader is over-represented in school suspensions and expulsion in the juvenile system. The shame of not learning to read as well as their peers drives them to high risks, and inappropriate behaviors, according to a Harvard University study in 2002, "On Race, Inequity in Special Education—A Shocking Trend in Our Nation's Public Schools."

In 1998, approximately 1.5 million minority children were identified as having mental retardation, emotional disturbance or a specific learning disability. The most distinguishable group, the dyslexic child, had language deficiencies as the root of the problem. Attempts to teach the children in the traditional way failed the dyslexic reader. They are underserved without specialized instruction and specialized methodology.

The National Association for the Education of African-American Children With Learning Disabilities Advocates "One Child at a Time."

Reading Is a Gift

Finally, we must remember that reading is a gift of humanity. Great pleasure is derived from the decoding of man's invention. The history of the English language is a fascinating study for all who love words. Those who have the powerful tools of reading must help those for whom the processing and using of words of our language is difficult.

All children have a desire to read. Observe the kindergartners as they imitate a true reader.

Dyslexia, may I repeat, though genetically influenced, does not spell biological failure. The failure lies with our educators, leadership

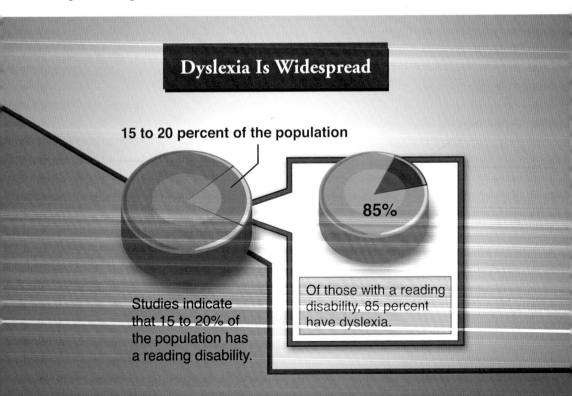

Dyslexia Is Widespread

15 to 20 percent of the population

85%

Studies indicate that 15 to 20% of the population has a reading disability.

Of those with a reading disability, 85 percent have dyslexia.

Taken from: Northern California Branch of the International Dyslexia Association, "Dyslexia Basics," 2000. www.dyslexia-ncbida.org.

and legislators, whose attitudes and policies toward inclusion of all children in the reading curriculum are abominable.

We cannot afford the continuous lack of vision. No child, dyslexic or otherwise, should "fall through the cracks." Dyslexia can be overcome with science based instruction methods.

EVALUATING THE AUTHOR'S ARGUMENTS:

After reading this viewpoint, what steps do you think the author would recommend to address the problem of dyslexia in schools?

Dyslexia Is Widely Misunderstood

David Mills

"Dyslexia carries so many wrong associations, and is understood in so many different ways . . . that it serves no useful scientific or therapeutic purpose."

In the following viewpoint David Mills argues that dyslexia is misunderstood by many people. Most of those labeled dyslexic, he asserts, are not significantly different from younger children who read at the same level. The scientific consensus indicates that the common understanding of dyslexia is erroneous. The term "dyslexia," he says, can be defined in so many ways that there is major disagreement about how or even whether the term should be used. Mills is a producer for Great Britain's Channel 4 *Dispatches* program, for which he produced the documentary *The Dyslexia Myth*.

AS YOU READ, CONSIDER THE FOLLOWING QUESTIONS:

1. According to Mills, how many initiatives has the British government introduced in primary schools?
2. In the author's view, what would happen if we tried to completely cease using the term dyslexia?
3. What would be the result, in Mills's view, if we used the term dyslexia to describe all children who have trouble reading due to phonological problems?

As a current affairs producer, every story you tell brings surprises. No story I have ever been involved with before though has produced as many eye-openers as the Channel 4 *Dispatches* programme *The Dyslexia Myth*.

There were numerous small revelations: ranging from the discovery that dyslexic children do not reverse their letters any more than younger children reading at the same level, to the discovery that the Government has so far introduced no fewer than 650 different initiatives in primary schools.

Then there were even more dramatic discoveries: poor readers with high IQs, usually seen as dyslexic, respond in exactly the same way to help with their reading as poor readers with low IQs who are rarely labelled as dyslexic.

Experts Agree Dyslexia Is a Myth

The biggest shock was that the 'dyslexia myth' story which sounded so controversial when I first started the research, turned out not to be controversial at all to the experts. The idea that the common understanding of dyslexia is a myth was startling when I first heard it. Yet I found it was a view shared by every academic that I talked to. The scientific consensus about it is overwhelming.

This poses two questions, both of which trouble me still, even though we did not deal with them in the documentary. I am raising them here in more detail. The first question is why has the story not been reported before? The second is what is the future of the term dyslexia?

An Underreported Story

The expert knowledge that the popular understanding of dyslexia [is] a 'myth', has been around for at least ten years. The research findings, taken collectively, are devastating. Yet they have never been properly reported to the public. Perhaps the reason for this is the inadequacy of the journalistic profession.

Or perhaps it reflects a bigger problem: a natural reluctance on the part of researchers to simplify and popularise the findings of other investigators. Although academics understand the big picture, few feel comfortable about dragging together all the different research findings

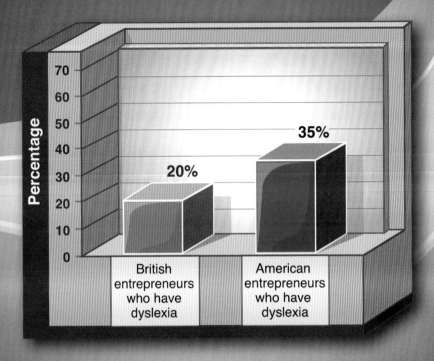

Many Entrepreneurs in the United States and England Have Dyslexia

20% British entrepreneurs who have dyslexia

35% American entrepreneurs who have dyslexia

Percentage (0, 10, 20, 30, 40, 50, 60, 70)

Taken from: Julie Logan, News-Medical.net, 2008. www.news-medical.net/?id=34153.

about a complex subject, simplifying them and putting them together to provide a simple overview. Academics are rated on their ability to come up with their own findings, not on how effective they are at popularising other people's research.

Defining Dyslexia

The question of how dyslexia could be defined generated a lot of controversy in the run up to the documentary. The reason we did not deal with it in the documentary is that there is simply too much disagreement about it. There are at least five major views about the future use of the term 'dyslexia':

View 1: The term dyslexia should be dropped completely. It is said that dyslexia carries so many wrong associations, and is understood in so many different ways by so many different people, that it serves no useful scientific or therapeutic purpose. It should be replaced by 'reading problems' or in more severe cases 'reading disability'.

I have a lot of sympathy with this view. As a journalist I like to know what words mean. There are problems though. The term dyslexia is so ingrained that a lot of people would still go on using it. There is also the fact that 'dyslexia' is a handy term for those trying to focus attention on the needs of those with reading problems.

View 2: 'Dyslexia' can be redefined to describe all children who find it difficult learning to read because of phonological problems. This would provide a clear definition which would identify children who have a sufficient problem detecting the smallest sounds in words which make learning to read difficult. It would thus identify children who will need additional tuition in a small group or even one-to-one help.

This could result in labelling up to one fifth of children as 'dyslexic'. Do we really want to suggest that so many children are in some way 'disabled'? Given that so many children have problems learning to read, we should look upon difficulty in learning to read as an entirely normal experience for quite a lot of children.

View 3: 'Dyslexia' should only be used to describe children with the severest problems. These children will need not only small group teaching but also often skilled one to one assistance to overcome their problem.

Such a definition has the merit that it would help institutions like the Dyslexia Institute focus attention on such children. Yet it would still label children as dyslexic who, with the right teaching at school, will learn to read perfectly well. It may also suffer from the difficulty of arriving at a cut off point. So on one side of this line a child would be labelled dyslexic, while on the other, a very similar child would not be.

View 4: 'Dyslexia' should be used only for the 1–2 per cent of children with a long-term reading problem who do not respond to the best school teaching currently possible. There is no doubt that these children need far more help than individual schools can provide, including diagnostic tests and long term support.

This view is supported by many leading researchers. It would mean that 'dyslexia' defines a clear group of children who are significantly disabled and for whom special help is both needed and justified.

View 5: 'Dyslexia' should no longer be really associated with reading problems nor defined in relation to reading. The argument is that there is a pattern disability, much wider than mere reading problems, which can be used to define who is, and who is not dyslexic.

The problem is that, as far as I am aware, there is precious little agreement on whether such a pattern exists or if it does exist, how at present it might be defined. There are indications that some adults who have suffered long-term reading disability do often share other problems, such as poor memory or poor organisational skills, but

The author of this viewpoint contends that only children with severe reading problems should be labeled dyslexic and receive special instruction in school.

whether this could be used to redefine dyslexia seems, on the evidence, problematic.

So what do I think after all the research that I have done? I am tempted by the definition in View 3, that dyslexia should be used to define children with the severest problems. However in the end I think I would come down in favour of View 4, reserving the term 'dyslexia' for the 1–2 per cent of children whose problems, on present evidence, are unlikely to be resolved by even the latest 'state of the art' school teaching. It would be a rigorous definition and focus attention on those who suffer most. They need all the help we can give them.

EVALUATING THE AUTHORS' ARGUMENTS:

Can this viewpoint, which asserts that experts agree that dyslexia is a myth, be reconciled with the previous viewpoint that dyslexia is a serious problem? On what points are the authors in agreement? Are their disagreements a matter of how the term "dyslexia" is used?

Attention Deficit Hyperactivity Disorder Is a Serious Problem

PR Newswire Contributor

"ADHD is a serious medical condition causing significant, life-long impairments."

In this viewpoint by PR Newswire contributor, Shire Pharmaceuticals Group, the author argues that attention deficit hyperactivity disorder (ADHD) not only affects quality of life but also costs billions of dollars every year. Though many associate ADHD with childhood problems, the effects of the disorder, says the author, continue well into adulthood. ADHD results in significantly less educational attainment, which, argues the author, lowers income. People with ADHD change jobs more frequently, miss more days of work, and are not able to work to full capacity. Shire is a global specialty pharmaceutical company.

PR Newswire Contributor, "$77 Billion in Lost Income Is Attributed to Attention-Deficit/Hyperactivity Disorder (ADHD) Annually in the U.S.," PR Newswire, May 23, 2005. Reproduced by permission.

U.S. household income losses due to attention-deficit/hyperactivity disorder (ADHD) total nearly $77 billion each year, according to a new analysis of the national large-scale survey, "Capturing America's Attention," presented [May 23, 2005] at the American Psychiatric Association (APA) annual meeting in Atlanta.

"ADHD, a life-long disorder, may be one of the costliest medical conditions in the United States," said Joseph Biederman, M.D., Professor of Psychiatry, Harvard Medical School and Chief of Pediatric Psychopharmacology at Massachusetts General Hospital. "The same ADHD symptoms that may cause young patients to perform poorly in school or miss classes may also cause these patients, as adults, to lose a significant amount of income each year. The compelling results of this survey show that ADHD is a serious medical condition causing significant, life-long impairments. Evaluating, diagnosing and treating this condition may not only improve the quality of life, but may save adults with ADHD billions of dollars every year."

ADHD Causes Income Loss

Biederman and his colleagues found that adults with ADHD have a lower educational attainment and achievement than healthy adults—factors that not only significantly impact employment rates and income, but cause difficulties in the workplace as well. But even when the investigators accounted for educational attainment and achievement, they found the average loss of household income per adult with ADHD ranged from $8,900 to $15,400 per year, depending on the econometric model used.

Over eight million adult Americans, or 4.3 percent of working-age adults, struggle with the inattention, impulsivity and hyperactivity of

ADHD. With this large-scale survey, researchers examined a weighted sample of 500 ADHD adults and 501 gender- and age-matched healthy adults that reflect the general U.S. population. They also accounted for personal and family characteristics, including characteristics closely tied to ADHD status, to arrive at the estimate of yearly household income losses due to the condition.

Barbara Eddy, an ADHD sufferer and working mom, like most people with ADHD, has a difficult time balancing work and family life and is susceptible to having "lost days."

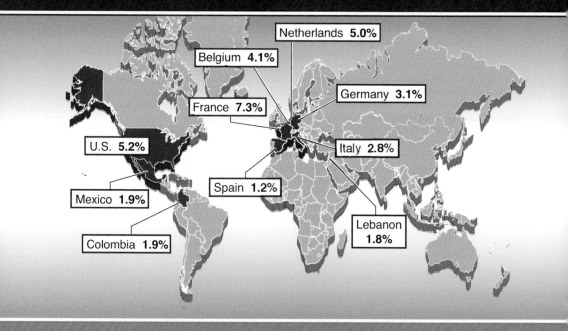

Netherlands 5.0%

Belgium 4.1%

Germany 3.1%

France 7.3%

U.S. 5.2%

Italy 2.8%

Mexico 1.9%

Spain 1.2%

Lebanon 1.8%

Colombia 1.9%

Taken from: WebMD Health News, May 27, 2008. www.webmd.com/add-adhd/news.

Nearly a quarter of the U.S. workforce (28 million workers ages 18 to 54) experience a mental disorder, according to a 2002 study by the University of Michigan. Employers are now starting to provide services that could be helpful to affected families including flexible work hours, family leave arrangements and childcare assistance, according to Dr. Biederman. Most employers offer employee assistance programs primarily targeted to helping employees deal with psychological issues, or work/life programs that focus on balancing work and family responsibilities.

ADHD Lowers Educational Attainment

According to the "Capturing America's Attention" survey results, adults with ADHD reported lower educational achievement and were less likely to be high school or college graduates. Higher education is associated with an expected higher income, and also is associated with higher rates of full-time employment. However, approximately 17 percent of the adults surveyed with ADHD did not graduate from high school, compared to 7 percent of those without ADHD. Similarly, just 19 percent of the adults with ADHD graduated from college compared to 25 percent of the adults without ADHD.

ADHD Reduces Employment, Increases Lost Days

In the survey, adults with ADHD had more jobs during the last 10 years, averaging 5.4 jobs compared to adults without ADHD, who had 3.4 jobs. Of those surveyed, only 52 percent of the adults with ADHD were currently employed, compared to 72 percent of the adults surveyed without ADHD. Among adults with ADHD who were currently employed and had more than one job in the last 10 years, 43 percent reported that they lost or left one or more of those jobs in some part because of their ADHD symptoms.

ADHD adults in the survey were three times more likely to suffer from stress, depression or other problems with emotion. These emotional and physical effects can cause people with ADHD to "lose" days of their lives, Biederman explains. "Lost days" may manifest as a day absent from work or several times throughout the month when the person is not fully engaged both physically and emotionally. About one in four (24 percent) adults with ADHD said that on 11 days per month, on average, they were

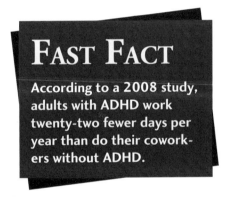

FAST FACT

According to a 2008 study, adults with ADHD work twenty-two fewer days per year than do their coworkers without ADHD.

prevented from normal activities such as work, due to poor mental or physical health, compared to only nine percent of the adults without ADHD.

The "Capturing America's Attention" survey was conducted among more than 1,000 adults aged 18 and older by Roper Public Affairs (formerly Roper ASW) via telephone interviews. The sample list was comprised of households where it was indicated in a health profile survey that there was a member in residence, at least 18 years of age or more, who had been diagnosed with ADHD. Shire US Inc. supported this survey.

ADHD Continues into Adulthood

Although many people tend to think of ADHD as a childhood problem, up to 65 percent of children with ADHD may still exhibit symptoms into adulthood, according to the National Institute of Mental Health. Although there is no cure for ADHD, physicians and advocates are finding ways to help people with the condition learn to adapt to their school, home, social and work settings. ADHD usually can be successfully managed with a combination of treatments, such as medication and structured coping techniques. Psychostimulants, medications that stimulate areas of the brain that control attention, impulses, and self-regulation of behavior, remain among the most successful treatments for people with ADHD. In fact, at least 70 percent of children with ADHD respond positively to psychostimulants. Medication should be considered part of an overall multi-modal treatment plan for ADHD.

> **EVALUATING THE AUTHOR'S ARGUMENTS:**
>
> This viewpoint was written by a pharmaceutical company that produces medications used to treat ADHD. How does that affect your assessment of the author's argument?

Viewpoint

4

Attention Deficit Hyperactivity Disorder Is a Myth

Fred A. Baughman Jr. and Craig Hovey

"The diagnostic criteria for ADHD ... are comprised of normal childhood behaviors."

Fred A. Baughman Jr. and Craig Hovey argue in this viewpoint that attention deficit hyperactivity disorder (ADHD) categorizes normal childhood behavior as a disease to be combated by drugging children to make them more submissive. According to the authors, the concept of "minimal brain dysfunction," which evolved into ADHD, is completely unscientific, and the criteria for diagnosing ADHD are far too broad. Parents have been misled by diagnoses of ADHD, they argue, as ADHD has no biological basis. Drugs like Ritalin, they say, are simply chemical restraints and schools have become drug pushers. Baughman is a neurologist for adults and children, and Hovey is a writer and economics teacher.

AS YOU READ, CONSIDER THE FOLLOWING QUESTIONS:
  1. According to the authors, what are the real reasons that children are forced to take drugs for ADHD?
  2. Why did the FDA ban the diagnosis of minimal brain dysfunction in 1979?
  3. According to figures cited by the authors, how many children today are being given Ritalin and other amphetamines to control behavior?

The discovery that amphetamines could be used to alter the behavior of children was made by accident in 1937. Charles Bradley was a physician at the Emma Pendleton Bradley Home in Rhode Island, a residential treatment center for children diagnosed with behavioral and neurological disorders. He observed the "calming" effect of stimulants on children when he gave Benzedrine (trademark for amphetamine) to a group of 30 children in order to treat headaches that resulted from spinal taps they were given. The Benzedrine did not do anything for the headaches, but it did make the children less active and more compliant, in a fashion he called "spectacular."

Drugging Unruly Children

In a chilling preview of the epidemic to come, he reported, "to see a single dose of Benzedrine produce a greater improvement in school performance than the combined efforts of a capable staff working in a most favorable setting, would have been all but demoralizing to the teachers had not the improvement been so gratifying from a practical viewpoint." In the years that followed, this anecdotal observation that stimulants have this effect was further reinforced and sparked the manufacture of both more drugs and the rationales necessary to justify giving them to troublesome children everywhere.

Nobody is going to come out and say that children should be forced to take speed and drugged into submission for the real reasons—it makes dealing with unruly children easier and a hugely profitable market exists for anything that can accomplish that feat. A diagnosible abnormality needed to be invented in order to provide the appearance of legitimate "treatment" being rendered in their best interests.

When Bradley further stated that, "It appears paradoxical that a drug known to be a stimulant should produce subdued behavior," he gave seed to the root of a misconception that continues to persist today, namely, that stimulants given to children labeled as ADHD affects them differently than normal people. The hope was that this would be so because a different reaction to the drugs could be used to help support the notion that there really was something wrong with the brains of ADHD labeled children that did not occur in the heads of normal kids. As further study revealed, however, these drugs have the same impact on just about anybody who gets them. The idea that something paradoxical was going on came from the fact that the "low" doses of amphetamines given to children increased their ability to focus on repetitive tasks and be compliant, just as happens to adults. It is at higher dosage levels that the effects more commonly associated with amphetamines (speed) occur.

In 1950 Dr. Bradley did another study with children, using Benzedrine (amphetamine) and Dexedrine (dextro-amphetamine). Of the 275 children given these, he reported between 60% and 70% to be much improved while on the drugs. Much improved meaning, as it does today, that their behavior became more appealing according to adult standards while under the influence of addictive drugs.

"Minimal Brain Dysfunction" Is an Unscientific Diagnosis

The best known of the stimulants given to children, methylphenidate (Ritalin), was synthesized by Ciba (a pharmaceutical company that later morphed into Novartis) in 1944, with its pharmacology described in 1954. In his excellent book, *The Creation of Psychopharmacology*, David Healy, M.D., tells us, "Later Leon Eisenberg used Ritalin in the first randomized controlled trial involving children, to test its effects on hyperactive states. It was effective and its effectiveness led to the acceptance of the concept of minimal brain dysfunction, which in 1980 in DSM-III became attention deficit disorder (ADD). Since then a growing, almost epidemic, use of Ritalin to treat this condition has become headline news."

Note the extremely important point made above by Healy; it was the drug's effectiveness that led to the acceptance of minimal brain dysfunction, the parent to ADD and ADHD. The fact that Ritalin worked in the same way on a particular group of children as it would

Drug Medication for ADHD Is Skyrocketing

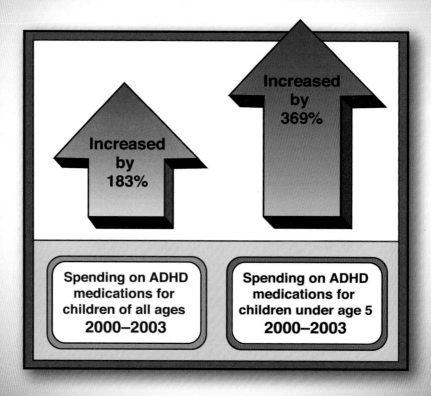

Increased by 183%

Increased by 369%

Spending on ADHD medications for children of all ages 2000–2003

Spending on ADHD medications for children under age 5 2000–2003

Taken from: WebMD Health News, May 17, 2004. www.webmd.com/baby/news.

on anybody was used to promote a diagnosis targeted at specific groups of (normal) children it claimed, as proponents of ADHD do today, had malfunctioning brains, as evidenced by their response to drug treatment. Is this just bad reasoning? Or was a deliberately deceitful strategy hatched to create patients and drug consumers where none should have existed?

The earliest precursor of ADHD came in the early 1900s when children who were unusually active, impulsive, or rebellious, might be diagnosed as having minimal brain damage, a term coined by Dr. George Still. The idea was that since brain damage can cause changes in behavior these children may have suffered some kind of assault on their brains. Indeed, a variety of conditions that damage the brain are associated with difficulties in attention and heightened activity levels, such as fetal alcohol syndrome or lead poisoning, but there is no meaningful correlation between known brain injuries or diseases in children and the inability to pay attention, sit still, or regulate one's impulses.

The minimal brain dysfunction label that came after Eisenberg's study of Ritalin removed the assumption of an injury to the brain and replaced it with the notion that something in the heads of these children was amiss, their brains somehow misfiring due to an abnormality they were born with, though nobody ever figured out what, or exactly where in the brain, it was. It was pure speculation with never a shred of scientific evidence to back it up. Hyperkinetic reaction was another label used in the 50s and 60s, though it never specified what was being reacted to and was simply a label for an active child in whom nothing verifiably wrong had been found.

ADD Is Typical Childhood Behavior

In 1979 the Food and Drug Administration ordered that minimal brain dysfunction be eliminated as a diagnostic term. They banished it because MBD was unscientific (had no grounding in facts). With symptoms of it no different than normal childhood behaviors, the diagnosis was rightly banished. Unfortunately, one bad idea was replaced by a worse idea, the creation of ADD, still completely unscientific but said to be an improvement because its diagnostic criteria were expanded and seemingly more specific. What this really did, however, was make it possible to include even more typical childhood behaviors under the diagnostic umbrella so that millions of normal children could be diagnosed and billions of dollars could be made off needlessly drugging them.

During the days of minimal brain dysfunction and hyperkinetic reaction the fields of psychology and psychiatry generally regarded children's problems as stemming from their environments, primarily as the result of faulty parenting. No matter what emotional or behavioral problems beset a person, so the reasoning went, the cause could be found in something that had gone wrong, or was going wrong, in childhood. Individuals were regarded as being in possession of naturally healthy brains, with rare exceptions of those with conspicuous brain damage, and only experienced psychological difficulties as the result of unhealthy experiences.

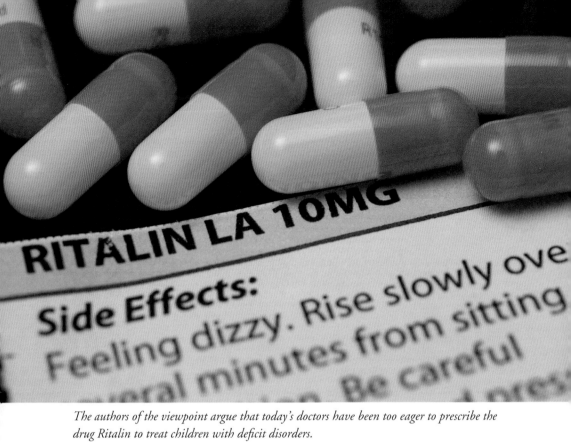

The authors of the viewpoint argue that today's doctors have been too eager to prescribe the drug Ritalin to treat children with deficit disorders.

Speculation About the Brain

In this kind of climate, viewing the behavioral problems of a child as being the result of defects within his own brain was a rare thing, which is why relatively few children were diagnosed with minimal brain dysfunction, or given behavior-modifying drugs. Things began to change late in the 60s, with a major shift obvious by the beginning of the 80s. Increasingly, psychiatry became a discipline where behavioral problems were seen as having biological rather than environmental roots, even though no proofs were ever produced for this shift in thinking. Now chemical imbalances and other forms of neurological abnormalities became the fashionable explanations. The contradiction right from the beginning was that, even though psychiatry increasingly claimed a biological basis for behavioral disorders, the discipline never produced any biological evidence to support its contentions. On one hand, psychiatry claims to be scientific, but on the other it has never produced evidence that passes scientific muster. What psychiatry has is a set of unsupported assumptions we are told to accept on faith, until the always-promised proof is discovered. In effect we are told to wait, like Charlie Brown sitting through the night in hopes of the Great Pumpkin's arrival.

Along with a different outlook on behavioral causes, in the past there was more understanding and tolerance for the normal range of childhood behaviors. Children vary greatly in interests, abilities, talents, and behavioral styles and this was commonly known and understood, as it is today when we choose to be reasonable about it. In the years since, with all the talk of diversity and the acceptance of differences among individuals, the tolerance for differences in how children act has plummeted. It used to be that the child who did poorly academically was understood to be somebody who would excel in other areas, where things like physical talent, creativity, personal skills, and the ability to switch gears quickly were called for, not the ability to sit still and obey directives.

Schools Become Drug Pushers

In 1961 Ritalin was approved by the Food and Drug Administration for use in children and remained, by today's standards, a drug not often employed, with the number of children taking it in 1970 being approximately 150,000. How did it go from that relatively low number to the over 6 million children today being given Ritalin and a variety of amphetamines? Lots of factors are involved, but the most obvious turning point came when schools began devoting themselves to identifying candidates for chemical restraint. And, as educators got better at it, psychiatry joined in by broadening the diagnostic criteria to the point where almost any

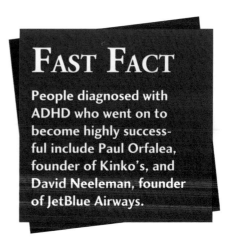

FAST FACT

People diagnosed with ADHD who went on to become highly successful include Paul Orfalea, founder of Kinko's, and David Neeleman, founder of JetBlue Airways.

child could be targeted for behavior modifying drugs. Along with them, pharmaceutical companies were quick to catch on to the huge market for stimulant drugs and went to great lengths to market the "disease" and their treatments for it. In speaking of pharmaceutical companies,

Dr. Healy points out that they have gone from barely existing prior to World War II to become ". . . giant corporations and the darlings of Wall Street . . . a medico-pharmaceutical complex that appears to have gradually shifted from discovering treatments for major diseases to medicalizing aspects of the human condition. We live in a Brave New World which is shaped not just by new drugs created in company laboratories, but by an almost Orwellian capacity to control the flow of information."

Parents Have Been Misled

Since 1970, parents have been flooded by misinformation from their schools, psychiatry, ADHD support groups, and the pharmaceutical companies, all telling them that even small deviations from narrow standards of behavior are evidence of a disease within the child, when none are—not a single one. Parents are also told these drugs are mild, safe, and effective. Of the two, the "disease" lie is absolute, in and of itself, abrogating the patient's right to informed consent.

It is interesting to note that as the definitions of, and criteria for MBD, ADD, and ADHD, were changed over the years, they became broader instead of more specific. How much of this was driven by the expanding knowledge of the impact of stimulants on children's behavior? Need one be paranoid to suspect that the diagnosis was broadened to accommodate a treatment that would "work" across the board?

ADHD Diagnosis Is Too Broad

Normally, as a condition is studied and more is learned about it, the diagnostic signs (signs=objective abnormalities) are narrowed down to a specific set of objective criteria that can be reliably applied. With ADHD the opposite happened, with more and more behaviors thrown into this free-for-all stew so that now it has become possible to pretty much drug any child who is not behaving or performing precisely as those with power over him want.

In their excellent book, *Coping with Children's Temperament*, William Carey, M.D., and Sean McDevitt, Ph.D., go into some of the problems with the ADHD label, saying ". . . our view is that the term ADHD is commonly used in the United States today to refer to an oversimplified grouping of a complex and variable set of normal but incompatible temperament variations, disabilities in cognition, problems in school function and behavior, and sometimes neurological immaturities. We believe that many different conditions are being called by this one name." If there is ever to be a legitimate label to denote a problem with attention, activity, or impulsivity, it will have to be much more specific and refer to a physical abnormality that can be identified objectively. This, after all, is the definition of disease.

ADHD Is Not a Disease

Carey and McDevitt talk about "when" ADHD is identified. But, precisely because the diagnostic criteria for ADHD . . ., are comprised of normal childhood behaviors, we see no reason for this optimism. If any true disease were to be discovered and verified that interferes with a child's ability to pay attention, control her activity levels, or reign in her impulsivity, it will have a scientific basis and objective means of identification. However, the American Psychiatric Association's DSM (Diagnostic and Statistical Manual) process of cobbling together subjective symptoms, voting on them, and calling them "diseases," bears no resemblance to the discovery of unique, new abnormalities (abnormality = disease) by observant physicians, and will never validate ADHD or any other psychiatric "disorder" as an actual disease.

EVALUATING THE AUTHORS' ARGUMENTS:

The author of the previous viewpoint recommended the prescription of medication to minimize the symptoms of ADHD; the authors of this viewpoint condemn the practice of medicating children for what they consider normal behaviors. Which argument do you find more persuasive? Cite examples from the texts to support your answer.

Autism Is a Serious Problem

Chris Emery

"Everyone is going to know someone who has a kid with autism."

In the following viewpoint Chris Emery asserts that autism is a serious problem. Children who suffer from autism, he writes, do not perceive and interact with the world in the way other children do and require special education services. Emery explains that although parents frequently notice symptoms of autism early in a child's life, a lag occurs between the time autism appears and the time it is diagnosed. An earlier diagnosis is important, he argues, because early treatment is the key to effectively dealing with autism. Emery writes for the *Baltimore Sun*.

AS YOU READ, CONSIDER THE FOLLOWING QUESTIONS:

1. According to the author, in the study of Maryland children, typically how much time passed between when parents noticed symptoms of autism and when autism was diagnosed?
2. At what age do many children benefit most from therapies designed to treat autism?
3. According to experts cited by the author, what behaviors are associated with autism spectrum disorder?

The most comprehensive study of autism to date shows that in Maryland and 13 other states the disorder is common and often diagnosed too late for effective therapies, according to the federal Centers for Disease Control and Prevention [CDC]. By analyzing youngsters' school and health records, the CDC found that one out of every 150 8-year-olds demonstrated symptoms of autism, a slightly higher rate than previous studies. The overall figure held as well for Maryland where the incidence rate of so-called autism spectrum disorders [ASDs] was in the middle of the 14 states surveyed. "Our estimates are becoming better and more consistent, though we can't yet tell if there is a true increase in ASDs or if the changes are the result of our better studies," said the CDC's director, Dr. Julie L. Gerberding. "We do know, however, that these disorders are affecting too many children.

Autism Is a Serious National Problem

Doctors and parents of autistic children seized on the figures as confirmation that autism is a serious national problem. "It's enormous. This suggests everyone is going to know someone who has a kid with autism," said Dr. Gary Goldstein, a pediatric neurologist and president and chief executive of the Kennedy Krieger Institute in Baltimore, which specializes in children's developmental disabilities. CDC researcher Catherine Rice cautioned against drawing national conclusions from the data because the states and subdivisions surveyed were not demographically representative of the entire country. But she said the consistency of the results from state to state was impressive. The study, which looked at autism rates in 2000 and 2002, also found Maryland children in the middle when it came to the age of diagnosis. The most recent survey, in 2002, looked at 407,578 8-year-olds in the 14 studied areas. On average, Maryland children were diagnosed with autism at 5 years of age—two years after parents typically begin to notice tell-tale symptoms of the disorder. Goldstein said he is concerned by delayed diagnosis because children often benefit most from therapies when they are 2 and 3 years old. "There was a three-year lag between parents coming in and saying there is a problem and the children actually being diagnosed" he said. "They missed an important window of opportunity."

Autistic Children Are Underserved

The researchers also looked at services available to autistic children in public schools. "People have historically criticized the availability of special education," Goldstein said. "But in kids with autism, if it's done right, it really helps." In 2002, some 74 percent of autistic children in Maryland received special education services in public schools, the highest proportion in the survey. The lowest was Colorado, where just 31 percent received services. Goldstein said the CDC data provide the most reliable estimate ever of autism rates in the United States—largely because researchers analyzed individual school and medical records to determine if children fit the criteria for an autism diagnosis. Previous studies found that 1 in every 166 children was autistic, he said, but their methodology was less rigorous. "This is the first time it was collected in a really uniform manner," he said. "This is the benchmark." The new study found that Alabama had the lowest rate of autism at 1 in 303 children in the age group. New Jersey had the highest rates, with one in every 94 children. There was no indication of why one state might be different from another—researchers said there could be environmental causes, or just more thorough screening in some jurisdictions than others.

FAST FACT

According to Steven Higgs of the *Bloomington Alternative*, the incidence of autism in Indiana as of early 2009 was 1 in 113 in school-age children. Thirty years ago, it was 1 in 5,000.

Difficulty with Social Interaction

Autism spectrum disorders in children are characterized by difficulty with social interaction and communication—often to the point where children are totally withdrawn from family and friends. "They do not perceive the world the way you or I do," said Elisa Hartman, of Towson, whose 6-year-old son Benjamin is autistic. "They need someone facilitating their interaction with the world." She first noticed the symptoms of the disorder in Benjamin when he was 2 years old. "He wasn't interested in the kinds of toys that other kids were interested in," she said. Benjamin became fascinated with making tubes out of paper and other materials, and he would play with the tubes for hours. He never pointed or waved goodbye—other common signs of the disorder. She said therapies have helped him develop physical and social skills, but he still has difficulty communicating. "You're doing all of the questioning, and he's only giving answers," she said. "And when he does ask a question he asks into the air, not looking at you."

She said her 2-year-old daughter, Zoey, has shown no signs of the disorder. (Boys are four times as likely to have an ASD than girls.)

Causes Unknown

Goldstein said some parents have blamed mercury-based preservatives sometimes used in vaccines for their children's autism but studies have found no scientific evidence to support the claim. "We don't know what causes it," Goldstein said. He added that research suggests many children who have the disorder probably inherit a predisposition for

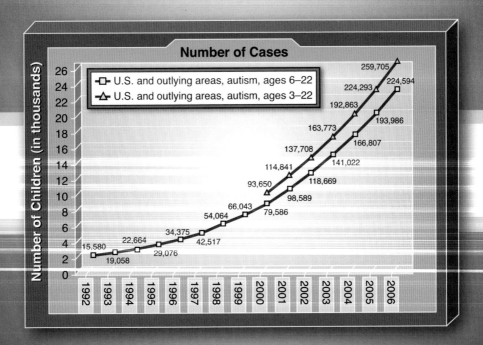

Increase in Autism Rates, 1992–2006

Taken from: FightingAutism, www.fightingautism.org/idea/autism.php.

it from their parents. The most suprising result of the new study, he said, was that many children are not being diagnosed until they enter kindergarten. He said he is cautiously optimistic that things may improve in the future, in part because Maryland legislators set aside money last year to encourage earlier detection of the disorder.

The funds, he said, are intended for programs to make pediatricians more aware of the symptoms of autism. "I don't know what it's

The author argues that autistic children require early diagnoses so that special education needs can be arranged and instituted.

like for 2- and 3-year-old children with autism right now," he said. "Hopefully it's better than it was in 2002." In addition to Maryland, the CDC study included Alabama, Arizona, Arkansas, Colorado, Georgia, Missouri, New Jersey, North Carolina, Pennsylvania, South Carolina, Utah, West Virginia and Wisconsin.

EVALUATING THE AUTHOR'S ARGUMENTS:

The author describes variations between states regarding the rates of autism reported. Which of the suggested explanations for the differences between states do you find most persuasive, and why?

Many Factors Have Contributed to the Rise in Autism Diagnoses

"The recent explosion of [autism] cases appears to be mostly caused by a surge in special education services for autistic children."

Mike Stobbe

Mike Stobbe argues in this viewpoint that autism rates are exaggerated. Rates of autism diagnoses have increased dramatically, but Stobbe asserts that behaviors now diagnosed as autism were just as common thirty or forty years ago. Broadening the definition of autism, he states, has caused the numbers to skyrocket. Stobbe claims that the main reason more children are diagnosed with autism is because the diagnosis will entitle them to special education services. Stobbe writes for the Associated Press.

AS YOU READ, CONSIDER THE FOLLOWING QUESTIONS:

1. According to the author, what motivates doctors and schools to diagnose children as having autism?

2. How has the rate of autism diagnosis changed in the last fourteen years, according to statistics cited by the author?
3. As autism rates have increased, how have rates for diagnoses of mild mental retardation changed, according to researchers cited by the author?

A few decades ago, people probably would have said kids such as Ryan Massey and Eddie Scheuplein were just odd. Or difficult.

Both boys are bright. But Ryan, 11, is hyper and prone to angry outbursts, sometimes trying to strangle another kid in his class who annoys him. Eddie, 7, has a strange habit of sticking his shirt in his mouth and sucking on it.

Both were diagnosed with a form of autism. And it's partly because of children such as them that autism appears to be skyrocketing: In the latest estimate, as many as one in 150 children have some form of this disorder. Groups advocating more research money call autism "the fastest-growing developmental disability in the United States."

Indeed, doctors are concerned there are even more cases out there, unrecognized: The American Academy of Pediatrics last week stressed the importance of screening every kid—twice—for autism by age 2.

Autism Formerly Characterized by Severe Impairments

But many experts believe these unsociable behaviors were just about as common 30 or 40 years ago. The recent explosion of cases appears to be mostly caused by a surge in special education services for autistic children, and by a corresponding shift in what doctors call autism.

Autism has always been diagnosed by making judgments about a child's behavior; there are no blood or biologic tests. For decades, the diagnosis was given only to kids with severe language and social impairments and unusual, repetitious behaviors.

Many children with severe autism hit themselves or others, don't speak and don't make eye contact. Blake Dees, a 19-year-old from Suwanee, Ga., falls into that group. For the past eight years, he has been in a day program with intense services, but he still doesn't

The author of the viewpoint believes that autism rates are exaggerated due to the need to get special education funding for autism treatment programs.

talk, he's not toilet-trained, and he has a history of trying to eat anything—even broken glass.

But he's not a typical case.

The Autism Umbrella

In the 1990s, the autism umbrella expanded, and autism is now shorthand for a group of milder, related conditions, known as "autism spectrum disorders." The spectrum includes Asperger's syndrome and something called PDD-NOS (for Pervasive Developmental Disorder—Not Otherwise Specified). Some support groups report more than half of their families fall into these categories, but there is no commonly accepted scientific breakdown.

Gradually, there have been changes in parents' own perception of autism, the autism services schools provide, and the care that insurers pay for, experts say.

Eddie, of Buford, Ga., was initially diagnosed with obsessive-compulsive disorder, attention deficit hyperactivity disorder and other conditions. But the services he got in school were not very helpful.

His mother, Michelle, said a diagnosis of autism brought occupational therapy and other, better services.

Diagnosis Is Given to Get Services

"I do have to admit I almost like the idea of having the autistic label, at least over the other labels, because there's more help out there for you," said Scheuplein.

"The truth is there's a powerful incentive for physicians and schools to classify children in a way that gets services," said Dr. Edwin Trevathan of the U.S. Centers for Disease Control and Prevention [CDC].

Many with Asperger's and PDD-NOS succeed in school and do not—at first glance—have much in common with children such as Mr. Dees.

At a recent gathering of families with Asperger's children in the Atlanta area, parents told almost comical stories about kids who frequently pick their noses, douse food in ketchup or wear the same shirt day after day. Such a frank, humorous exchange was once a rarity. Doctors for many years believed in the "refrigerator mom" theory, which held that autism was the result of being raised by a cold, unloving mother. The theory became discredited, but was difficult to dislodge from the popular conscience.

Even in the early 1980s, some parents were more comfortable with a diagnosis of mental retardation than autism, said Trevathan, director of the CDC's National Center on Birth Defects and Developmental Disabilities. Today, parents are more likely to cringe at a diagnosis of mental retardation, which is sometimes equated to a feeble-mindedness and may obscure a child's potential.

Autism Has Become Culturally Acceptable

And increasingly, professionals frown at the term: The special education journal *Mental Retardation* this year changed its name to *Intellectual & Developmental Disabilities*. The editor said that "mentally retarded" is becoming passe and demeaning, much as the terms idiot, imbecile and moron—once used by doctors to describe varying degrees of mental retardation.

In contrast, autism has become culturally acceptable—and a ticket to a larger range of school services and accommodations. In 1990, Congress added the word "autism" as a separate disability category to a federal law that guarantees special education services, and Education Department regulations have included a separate definition of autism since 1992.

Before that, children with autism were counted under other disabling conditions, such as mental retardation, said Jim Bradshaw, an education department spokesman.

The Social Security Administration also broadened its definition of disability to include spectrum disorders, such as Asperger's.

Something else changed: The development of new stimulants and other medicines may have encouraged doctors to make diagnoses with the idea of treating them with these drugs.

Numbers Increase Due to Services Categorization

Perception of the size of the problem changed, too. Fourteen years ago, only 1 in 10,000 children were diagnosed with it. Prevalence estimates gradually rose to the current government estimate of one in 150.

That increase has been mirrored in school districts. Gwinnett County Public Schools—Georgia's largest school system—had eight classrooms for teaching autistic youngsters 13 years ago; today there are 180.

Some researchers suggest that as autism spectrum diagnoses have gone up, diagnoses of mild mental retardation have fallen. U.S. Department of Education data show that the number of students with autism rose steadily, from about 42,500 in 1997 to nearly 225,000 in 2006. Meanwhile, the number of students counted as mentally retarded declined from about 603,000 to about 523,000.

FAST FACT

A 2004 Australian study found that 58 percent of the doctors surveyed admitted that they have been exaggerating the diagnosis of autism in children in order to help families get access to assistance at home and in schools.

CDC scientists believe education numbers are misleading, because they reflect only how kids are categorized for services. They say there's no clear evidence doctors are substituting one diagnosis for the other.

Some parents believe environmental factors—ranging from a preservative in vaccines to contaminants in food or water—may be important contributors. (The last doses of early childhood vaccines

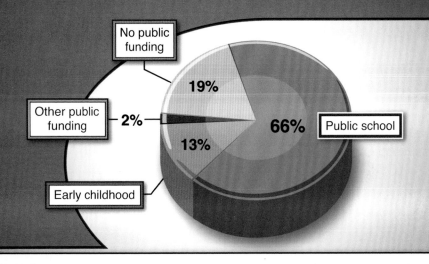

Funding for Speech and Language Therapy

This chart shows the percentage of families participating in the Interactive Autism Network (IAN) who benefit from some sort of public funding for speech and language therapy.

No public funding

19%

Other public funding   2%

13%

66%   Public school

Early childhood

Taken from: Interactive Autism Network, "IAN 'Back to School' Report," August 25, 2008. www.iancommunity.org.

containing the preservative thimerosal expired in 2002, although some children's flu shots still contain it.)

Some of the Increase Is Real

Dr. Gary Goldstein, scientific adviser to the national advocacy group Autism Speaks, said the explanation for the rising autism prevalence is probably complex. Labeling and diagnosing probably play a role, as do genetics, but he believes the increase surpasses those two explanations.

"I'm seeing more children with autism than I ever would have expected to see," said Dr. Goldstein, who is chief executive of the Kennedy Krieger Institute, a treatment center for pediatric developmental disabilities in Baltimore.

Autism Speaks budgets more than $4 million each year to research the causes of autism, and about 90 percent of that has gone to genetics research. But organization officials recently have been talking about changing that mix, and spending as much as 50 percent of that money on potential environmental triggers, Goldstein said.

Whether it's because of genes or the environment (or both), autism has hit the Massey family hard. Chuck and Julia Massey, of Dacula, Ga., have three sons with Asperger's.

The youngest, Ryan, was first diagnosed after he was slow to develop speaking ability. His brothers—Trevor, 14, and Morgan, 16—had learning and behavior problems and were later diagnosed with Asperger's, too. All got special education services and were treated with medications. Morgan has improved, or matured, or both, and is now a social kid in mainstream classes at a Gwinnett County high school. Trevor seems to be making the same transition, his mother said.

Ryan is the most extreme. He still has uncontrollable tantrums and must attend an Asperger's-only sixth-grade classroom that teaches social skills along with traditional subjects.

In a recent interview at the family's home, Ryan acknowledged he still has anger control issues. One of the three other students in his class is particularly irritating. Ryan said the way he reacts is by "grabbing his throat."

But on this night, Ryan was calm. He described himself as happy, and paced the room telling jokes, like a nervous stand-up comedian. ("Why didn't the skeleton go to the party? He didn't have the guts," he said, eyes fixed on his audience.)

Having three Asperger's boys under one roof has at times been very intense, Mrs. Massey said, noting a replaced dining room window.

Ryan acknowledged it's been educational living in a house full of Asperger's kids. Asked to name something he's learned from his brothers, he replied, "Swears."

EVALUATING THE AUTHORS' ARGUMENTS:

After reading this article and the one preceding it, which author do you think best supports his argument regarding the incidence of autism? Give reasons for your answers.

Autism Disabilities Vary Greatly

Robert Nohle

"Autism can be a confusing diagnosis because the behaviors and degrees of disability can vary greatly."

In the following viewpoint Robert Nohle explains that the disabilities associated with autism vary greatly. He contends that some people with autism are relatively high functioning, while others are severely disabled. While the classic form of autism often includes severe restriction of language development, he explains, other types of autism, such as Asperger's syndrome, may not have any general language delay. The author states that some types of autism do not fit into any category. Medications can treat some of the symptoms of autism and specialists can provide treatment, but there is no cure for the various types of autism. Nohle is chief of pediatrics for Seattle-based Group Health Cooperative.

AS YOU READ, CONSIDER THE FOLLOWING QUESTIONS:

1. By what age is the "classic" form of autism almost always present in children who have it?
2. What terms are used to categorize children who do not meet the criteria of other categories of autism?
3. While children with Asperger's may have good language skills, why might they still have trouble communicating, according to the author?

The word autism conjures up several different images for many parents. Some might think of Dustin Hoffman's character in *Rain Man*. Others may picture a child continually banging his head against a wall. Still others may think of an autistic person who is unexplainably and extraordinarily talented as a musician or artist.

Autism Varies Greatly

Autism can be a confusing diagnosis because the behaviors and degree of disability can vary greatly. Some people with autism are relatively

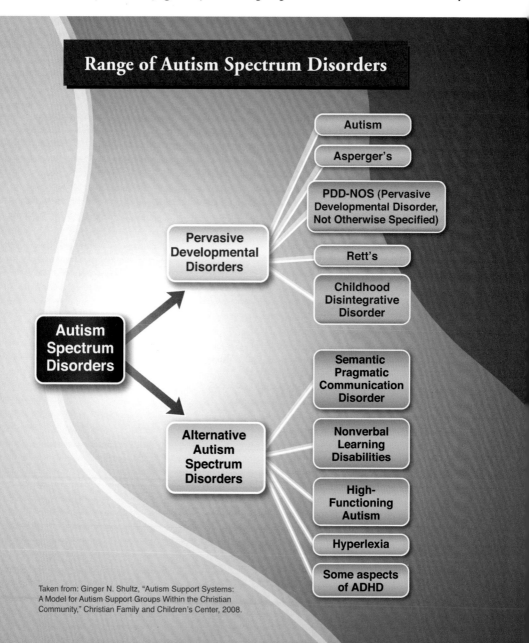

Range of Autism Spectrum Disorders

Autism Spectrum Disorders

Pervasive Developmental Disorders
- Autism
- Asperger's
- PDD-NOS (Pervasive Developmental Disorder, Not Otherwise Specified)
- Rett's
- Childhood Disintegrative Disorder

Alternative Autism Spectrum Disorders
- Semantic Pragmatic Communication Disorder
- Nonverbal Learning Disabilities
- High-Functioning Autism
- Hyperlexia
- Some aspects of ADHD

Taken from: Ginger N. Shultz, "Autism Support Systems: A Model for Autism Support Groups Within the Christian Community," Christian Family and Children's Center, 2008.

high functioning, with speech and intelligence intact. Others are mentally retarded, mute, or have serious language delays. Some people with autism seem closed off and shut down; others seem locked into repetitive behaviors and rigid patterns of thinking.

Autistic disorder is characterized by impairments in three areas: communication, socialization and imaginative play.

The "classic" form of autism most always is present by age 3— with most children showing signs between the ages of 15 to 24 months. Classic autism often includes severe restriction of language development.

FAST FACT

Approximately 10 percent of persons with autistic disorder also have some special skills in areas such as math calculations, art, or music.

Asperger's Syndrome

A more common type of autism, most often diagnosed in school-age children, is Asperger's Syndrome. Asperger's shares the same features of autism but to a lesser degree. Their intelligence typically is average to above average and typically there is not a general language delay.

The terms "autism spectrum disorder" or "pervasive developmental disorder not otherwise specified" are used to categorize children who do not meet the criteria for one of the other categories of autism. Across the entire autism spectrum, a small percentage of children have some special skill at a much higher level than the rest of their abilities—in such fields as art, music, mathematics or memory.

Children with Asperger's may have good language skills, yet still have trouble communicating. They don't always pick up on non-verbal signs and have trouble reading social cues.

For example, I once was talking with a mom of an 11-year-old child with Asperger's. Out of nowhere her child said, "Dr. Nohle, your nose is sure big." Whether or not this is the truth (hmmm), it was irrelevant to what was going on and inappropriate. It is that kind of inappropriateness that can make it very hard for children with Asperger's to develop friendships.

In fact, often parents will come to me with unspecific concerns such as their child has problems with relationships, has a strange or

Children with Asperger's syndrome sometimes have good language skills but cannot pick up on nonverbal communication signs from others and have trouble reading social cues.

narrow range of interests or is just "different." This type of behavior, combined with a thorough health history, raises the suspicion of an Asperger's diagnosis.

Difference in the Brain Causes Autism

Autism spectrum disorders are the result of biologic or neurologic differences in the brain; it is not a mental illness. What makes this especially frustrating for parents is that we are not sure what causes autism and there is no "cure." Autism can run in families, so many researchers think there likely is a genetic element.

We are more sure of what does not cause autism. There is no known psychological cause. Autism is not caused by post-traumatic syndrome or stress. There is also no known relationship between immunizations and autism. I realize that this may be a controversial statement to some parents.

Parents will bring this up to me, but I have to tell them that immunizations are one of the most studied areas of pediatric medicine. No link has ever been found, not even remotely, that immunizations—or mercury previously used in immunizations—causes autism. There just isn't the data to support a link.

No Miracle Cure

Once an autistic disorder is diagnosed, treatment usually is provided through a number of specialists depending on the child's needs: occupational and physical therapists, psychologists, psychiatrists, pediatrician and perhaps a neurologist. Medications can be prescribed to target some of the symptoms of autism, such as aggression, attention deficit, and obsessive compulsiveness, but they do not cure it.

I need to caution parents to be careful when doing research on treatments or miracle cures for autism. The Internet is rife with both bad information and people out to make a dollar on another's suffering. Your child's physician is there to help you navigate the information. It is his or her job to ensure that your child is getting the most appropriate treatment.

I understand that some parents can feel so hopeless that they want to do something, but you need to make sure you are helping rather than hurting.

EVALUATING THE AUTHOR'S ARGUMENTS:

If autism has so many variations, what do you think the author would say are characteristics common to all autism disorders? Identify parts of the viewpoint that support your answer.

Chapter 2

What Harm Is Caused by Disabilities Affecting Learning?

A large majority of learning-disabled children have behavioral and emotional problems that often lead to substance abuse.

Learning Disabilities Cause Behavioral Problems

Viewpoint 1

"Adolescents with learning disabilities frequently exhibit co-occurring emotional and behavioral problems."

Diana Mahoney

In the following viewpoint Diana Mahoney asserts that learning disabilities create a psychological burden on students that affects their behavior. She contends that an abnormally high percentage of students with learning disabilities have behavioral and emotional problems. Students with learning disabilities are more likely to drop out of school and engage in risky behavior. Intervention can help, she contends, but schools need to be more aware of the behavioral problems associated with learning disabilities. Mahoney writes for *Clinical Psychiatry News*.

AS YOU READ, CONSIDER THE FOLLOWING QUESTIONS:

1. According to studies cited by the author, how do the rates of emotional distress in students with learning disabilities compare to rates in students without learning disabilities?
2. What percentage of learning-disabled children have behavioral and emotional problems, according to data cited by the author?
3. According to the author, how much more likely are high school dropouts, as compared to graduates, to have trouble with the law?

Diana Mahoney, "Social and Emotional Costs of Learning Disabilities," *Clinical Psychiatry News*, February 1, 2008. Copyright © 2008 International Medical News Group. Reproduced by permission.

T he notion that learning disabilities are an academic problem
exclusively is not only erroneous, it's dangerous. The strug-
gles of children with impairments in reading, writing, math,
memory, and organization extend far beyond the classroom and often
contribute to a heavy psychological burden.

The Learning Disabled Have More Behavioral Problems

Multiple studies demonstrate that adolescents with learning disabilities
frequently exhibit co-occurring emotional and behavioral problems,
including depression, anxiety, conduct disorders, and delinquency.
In the landmark 2001 National Longitudinal Study of Adolescent
Health, a cross-sectional analysis of the in-home interview data of
more than 20,000 adolescents included in the study showed that rates
of emotional distress, suicide attempts, and involvement in violence
were significantly increased in the 1,301 adolescents who were identified as having a learning disability, compared with their non–learning
impaired peers. Similar results have been reported in a variety of community and clinical samples.

As many as 20% of people in the United States have a learning disability (including about 3 million children aged 6–21 years
who receive special education services in school), and about 30% of
learning-disabled children have behavioral and emotional problems,
according to data presented in the Department of Education's 2005
report to Congress on the Individuals With Disabilities Education
Act. The lesson? The societal impact of this problem is huge.

In the 2003 National Survey of Children's Health, learning disabilities were the most commonly diagnosed emotional, developmental,
or behavioral problem of children aged 0–17 years. Compared with
their peers without developmental problems, these children had lower
self-esteem, had more depression and anxiety, and missed more school
and were less involved in sports and other community activities.

More Likely to Drop Out of School

In addition, children with learning disabilities drop out of high
school at a disproportionately higher rate than their peers, and high
school dropouts are 3.5 times more likely to have trouble with the
law than are those who graduate, according to the National Center
for Educational Statistics.

Literature on the causal direction of the co-occurrence of behavioral/ emotional and learning problems is inconsistent. For example, it is unclear whether learning impairments beget mental health troubles or vice versa, whether the causation is reciprocal, or whether a shared etiologic factor [a factor related to cause] underlies the overlap. It is clear, however, that "a cascade of negative psychosocial effects occur

Studies have shown that teens with learning disabilities or ADHD are significantly more likely to abuse alcohol.

with learning disabilities," said David Osher, Ph.D., project director for the American Institutes for Research in Washington.

Adult expectations of adolescents make them particularly vulnerable to negative sequelae [conditions resulting from a disorder or event], contends John McNamara, Ph.D., associate professor in the department of child and youth studies at Brock University in St. Catharines, Ont. A younger child with a learning disability who exhibits a behavioral need probably would be identified in elementary school, but a teenager at risk for emotional or behavioral problems "is operating within a setting where expectations shift to the adolescents advocating for themselves—so a kid in trouble can fall off the radar," he said.

Learning Disabled and Risky Behavior

In a large-scale study published in 2005, Dr. McNamara and his colleagues explored the relationship in adolescents between learning disabilities and risk-taking behavior. They determined that adolescents with learning disabilities (and adolescents with learning disabilities and comorbid attention-deficit hyperactivity disorder) were significantly more likely to smoke, use alcohol and marijuana, engage in acts of direct aggression, and engage in acts of minor delinquency.

In a recent follow-up to that study, which is slated for publication this summer [2008], Dr. McNamara said he and his colleagues asked why adolescents with learning disabilities engage in these risk-taking activities to a greater extent than their non-learning disabled peers. The investigators found support for their hypothesis that psychosocial factors partly mediate the link.

Among the mediating psychosocial covariates [variables that affect psychological and social well-being] were adolescents' familial relationships, engagement in school and extracurricular activities, and feelings of well-being and of being victimized. "To us, these findings support the idea that it is a combination of the learning disability, per se, and the secondary psychosocial characteristics associated with adolescents with learning disabilities that explains the more frequent engagement in risk taking," he said.

The findings also show that "these kids require someone to step into their space to ensure they're thriving."

Intervention Can Help

These adolescents can thrive, Dr. McNamara stressed. "It is evident in the research that successful adolescents with learning disabilities are self-aware and have accepted their learning disability. They have learned to seek support when they need it, and they have learned to seek out and operate in environments where they have the tools to succeed," he said. "The ability to do these things comes from someone teaching them how to do so through well-designed interventions."

The key components to effective intervention for these adolescents, according to Dr. McNamara, include "intensive intervention during the early school years; ongoing one-on-one, or close to it, tutoring; consistent academic and life skill-based counseling; and consistent ongoing parental support and understanding."

> **FAST FACT**
>
> Recent studies indicate that between 30 percent and 70 percent of children with ADHD continue to exhibit symptoms in their adult years.

Feeling a sense of connectedness to and support from school also serves as an important protective factor, according to the findings of the adolescent health survey. Adolescents who receive such support "often have higher self-esteem, feel more in control of their own academic achievement, and understand how to advocate for themselves," Dr. McNamara said.

Schools Need to Be More Aware

To best serve not only the academic needs of adolescents with learning disabilities but also the social and emotional ones, educators and mental health providers first must understand "that the co-occurrence of behavioral and emotional problems with learning disabilities is common and leads to poorer outcomes," according to Dr. Osher. Next, they must work together to create emotionally safe and supportive school environments.

Also, "the interventions should be culturally and linguistically competent, strengths based, capacity building, and as child and family

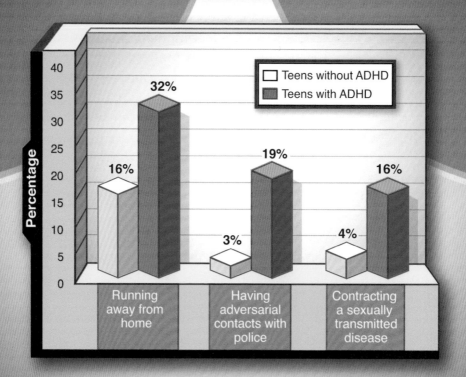

Behavioral Issues Among Teens with and Without ADHD

Percentage

- Teens without ADHD
- Teens with ADHD

40
35
30
25
20
15
10
5
0

16% / 32% — Running away from home

3% / 19% — Having adversarial contacts with police

4% / 16% — Contracting a sexually transmitted disease

Taken from: Susan Ashley, *The ADD & ADHD Answer Book.* Naperville, IL: Sourcebooks, Inc., 2005.

driven as possible," Dr. Osher said. "Wherever possible, labeling and pullout approaches and special classes should be avoided."

But multiple barriers impede the development of such emotionally safe and supportive learning environments. Problematic are disinterest, lack of information about what to do and how to do it, and the pressures faced by school administrators to produce "short-term gains on high-stakes tests," Dr. Osher said. "What gets assessed gets addressed," he said, so if schools are to become a protective factor in the lives of at-risk kids, social and emotional considerations must be assessed.

Strategies and Funding Are Needed

Toward this end, Dr. Osher and colleagues at the American Institutes for Research, together with the Collaborative for Academic, Social, and Emotional Learning and the Learning First Alliance, developed a strategy for overcoming barriers. The three-component intervention, which has been implemented by the Chicago Public Schools, includes a psychometrically robust 57-item survey of the social and emotional conditions for learning, the results of which are incorporated into school, district, or state score cards; a customized report informing administrators on the significance of specific subgroup responses to the survey; and an online tool kit linked to individual school reports that provides strategies and programs that have proven effective in similar contexts.

In Chicago, the results of the survey reports have begun to change discourse in the district, Dr. Osher reported. Still, several barriers to widespread implementation and efficacy of such strategies have yet to be overcome. For example, Dr. Osher said, the ongoing "marginalization of social [and] emotional factors" makes it difficult to generate financial resources for comprehensive assessments and intervention design.

And even when financial support exists, "another barrier is making sure that interventions enter the classroom, affect the learning process, and reach the individual child. This is a struggle in all systems change, including education."

EVALUATING THE AUTHOR'S ARGUMENTS:

The author says that studies are conflicting regarding whether learning problems cause psychological problems or vice versa. Do you think it is important to know the answer to this question? Do you think the author would say that it is important? Why or why not?

Viewpoint 2

Children with Learning Disabilities Are Vulnerable to Abuse

Freda Briggs

"Children with learning disabilities [are vulnerable] to the risks of drugs, violence, psychological bullying, pornography, sexual abuse and other safety hazards."

Freda Briggs argues in this viewpoint that having a learning disability makes a child more likely to be a victim of violence, sexual abuse, and other hazards. Citing prior studies and the results of her own study, Briggs contends that learning disabilities make children more vulnerable to abuse both at school and at home. Learning disabled children, she says, need assistance in protecting themselves from older and more powerful perpetrators. Briggs is a professor emerita of child development.

AS YOU READ, CONSIDER THE FOLLOWING QUESTIONS:

1. According to statistics cited by the author, how does the likelihood that a severely learning disabled child will be sexually abused compare to that of other children?

2. How likely are learning disabled children to discuss safety issues with parents, compared with non-LD children?
3. In the present study, how does the likelihood that a learning disabled child will experience violence vary depending upon whether the child is in a special education unit versus mainstream school?

Quantitative and qualitative data were collected from 116 special education students aged 11–17 years (61 females and 55 males) who had been identified as 3 or more years behind their peers in all aspects of the curriculum. The study confirmed the vulnerability of children with learning disabilities to the risks of drugs, violence, psychological bullying, pornography and sexual abuse. Significant levels of violence were found in both schools and homes. The study also showed the need for special attention for the protection of boys. It is possible that children with learning disabilities were targeted because they were less likely than others to (a) recognise abuse as wrong, (b) understand their rights and report abuse, and (c) be regarded as competent witnesses for court proceedings. On the other hand, it is possible that they were learning-disabled as a result of abuse. The findings suggested that children with learning disabilities require more vigilant and more intensive, explicit forms of protection than other children.

Danger to LD Children Has Been Known for Some Time

The particular vulnerability of children with disabilities to all forms of abuse was brought to public notice in the 1980s. American and Canadian studies suggested that these children are up to seven times more likely to be sexually abused than their non-disabled peers.

The literature suggests that children with disabilities are at highest risk of all forms of abuse because they are devalued by society in general. They were found to be the least well informed about their rights, their sexuality and the limits of acceptable social behaviour. They are inadequately protected by the justice system and child welfare agencies and lack self-esteem and the confidence to complain. Furthermore, there is a high risk that abuse will continue

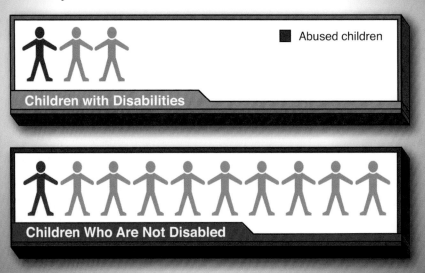

Abuse of the Disabled

According to the Agency for Persons with Disabilities, one out of every three children who has a disability is abused, and one out of every ten children who is not disabled is abused.

Abused children

Children with Disabilities

Children Who Are Not Disabled

Taken from: Agency for Persons with Disabilities, State of Florida.
http://apd.myflorida.com/zero-tolerance/overview.htm.

into adulthood. Research . . . showed that the victimization of children with disabilities compounds the low self-esteem, emotional problems, sense of helplessness, frustration, anger, depression, fearfulness and withdrawal associated with their disabilities. . . .

[One study] evaluated the curriculum with 252 intermediate school children aged 11 and 12 years and their parents in both North and South Islands [of New Zealand]. Children identified as having severe learning problems were at greatest risk of all forms of abuse and exposure to illegal drugs, pornography (63% versus 24% of others), drug abuse (50% versus 12%) and sexual abuse (81% versus 4%). Eighty-one per cent of girls in special education groups for learning disabilities had previously reported substantiated sexual offences committed by from two to 10 offenders before the age of 11. In all cases, students had been shown pornography to stimulate their curiosity, desensitize them and normalize deviant sex. . . .

Adults Not Protecting LD Children

Although the school programme has parent participation built into it, children with learning disabilities were the ones least likely to have had any conversations with parents about personal safety issues (44% versus 82% of others). Clearly, it is more difficult for staff to communicate effectively with parents if children travel by school bus. Communications are even harder to achieve if parents also have learning disabilities and are illiterate. Most abuse was committed by mothers' boyfriends, siblings and uncles. Only one student in this group was sexually abused by her biological father. The low rate of father-daughter incest could possibly be explained by the fact that most students in this group had little or no contact with their fathers.

The researchers were concerned about the safety of boys, many of whom stated that child protection programmers were irrelevant to them because only girls and homosexuals are sexually abused. A previous study of safety issues for New Zealand secondary students supported these concerns and also showed that boys would be afraid to disclose abuse by males because of confusion about their sexuality, embarrassment and the fear of (a) being disbelieved; (b) violent retribution and (c) being labeled as gay and bullied by peers.

Children Chosen for This Study

Because of the finding that girls with learning disabilities were so highly vulnerable to drug and sexual abuse and violence, the present study was extended in 2003/2004 to examine more closely safety issues affecting children with learning disabilities (both boys and girls).

One hundred and sixteen subjects (all the available students) were interviewed individually in special education centres using [a] 1996 questionnaire designed for intermediate school children. Issues for boys were then compared with issues for girls.

The period of time that subjects had spent in special education ranged from five weeks to two years. Before that, all subjects previously attended mainstream schools in both the North and South Islands of New Zealand. A few older respondents continued to attend the local mainstream school in a part-time capacity. All participants had an individually designed curriculum to cater for the fact that they were at least three years behind their chronological age group in all areas. Some were diagnosed as having ADD or ADHD, one with Down Syndrome, and one was brain damaged as a result of physical abuse in infancy. Some had minor intellectual disabilities. The ages of respondents ranged from 11 to 17 years. . . . There were slightly more girls (61, or 53%) than boys (55, or 47%). . . .

Violence Against LD Children

Students were asked to assess and compare the levels of violence experienced in special education units versus mainstream schools. Although some had anger management problems requiring medication, children with learning disabilities said they experienced more violence in mainstream schools (47%) than in separate single-sex special education centres (34%). There were no sex differences on this variable.

One-quarter of respondents thought there was a lot of violence in their own homes. Males were reported as being the most frequent users of physical violence against children with learning problems in the family home.

Learning-disabled children are less likely to report physical or sexual abuse than children without disabilities.

Children gave various reasons for why they were hit at home. There were no consistent sex differences in the pattern revealed. These children with special needs were shown to be very vulnerable to the aggression of irritable adults and siblings. . . .

Bullying at School

Although bullying was considered to be a big problem for many children with learning disabilities in special education (38%), it was more frequently perceived to be a problem when they attended a mainstream school (56%).

Name-calling and teasing were most frequently identified by girls (60%) and boys (57%) as the

> **FAST FACT**
>
> Research has estimated that 90 percent of people with developmental disabilities will experience sexual violence at some point during their lives.

most distressing form of bullying. Spreading false, unpleasant, sex-related rumours (such as "She's got AIDS", "She's a lesbian", "She's a prostitute", "She's promiscuous") and insults relating to body appearance (fat, ugly) were twice as prevalent among girls (13%) than boys (6%), who were usually referred to as "poofter" or homosexual to create distress.

Drugs, Abduction, and Sexual Abuse

Boys were significantly more likely to have been offered various major types of drugs than girls.

Almost two-thirds of the students (63%) reported having seen hardcore pornography. Magazines and videos were the most frequent source of such material.

Twenty cases (or 17%) reported that a stranger had tried (unsuccessfully) to persuade them to accompany them. There was no significant difference in the frequency with which this had happened to boys and to girls. The common theme for both girls and boys was an attempt by a male stranger to get the children into their car.

While school counsellors indicated that 44% of girls were victims of (substantiated) sexual abuse, only 32% of female respondents disclosed these offences to researchers. . . .

LD Children Must Be Protected

The study confirmed the vulnerability of children with learning disabilities to the risks of drugs, violence, psychological bullying, pornography, sexual abuse and other safety hazards. The study showed significant levels of violence in both schools and homes. This presents challenges to finding ways of assisting children to protect themselves against older and more powerful perpetrators.

EVALUATING THE AUTHOR'S ARGUMENTS:

Given the data presented by the author, what do you think accounts for the differences between safety risks LD children experience in mainstream schools compared with those in special education units?

Viewpoint

3

Autism Is Linked to Changes in the Brain

"Social fear in autism [causes an] adaptation that kills amygdala cells and shrinks the structure."

National Institutes of Health

In this viewpoint from the National Institutes of Health, the author argues that the social fear experienced by autistic children triggers a reaction that ultimately causes brain cells to die in the amygdala, the brain's "fear hub." Shrinkage of this part of the brain, the author contends, is linked to impaired nonverbal social behavior in childhood. Persons with smaller amygdalae have more difficulty recognizing emotional expressions and avoid looking at others in the eye. The National Institutes of Health, a part of the U.S. Department of Health and Human Services, investigates causes, treatments, and cures for diseases.

AS YOU READ, CONSIDER THE FOLLOWING QUESTIONS:

1. According to the author, how does social fear in autism initially affect the amygdala part of the brain?
2. According to study results cited by the author, how did autistic subjects with the smallest amygdalae compare to those with the largest amygdalae in the time it took to recognize emotion in facial expressions?

U.S. Department of Health and Human Services, National Institutes of Health Contributor, "Brain's Fear Center Shrinks in Autism's Most Severely Socially-Impaired," *NIH News,* December 4, 2006.

3. According to study results cited by the author, how much longer did autistic subjects with the larger amygdalae spend looking at the eyes of other persons, compared to those with the smaller amygdalae?

The brain's fear hub likely becomes abnormally small in the most severely socially impaired males with autism spectrum disorders, researchers funded by the National Institutes of Health's (NIH) National Institute of Mental Health (NIMH) and National Institute on Child Health and Human Development (NICHD) have discovered. Teens and young men who were slowest at distinguishing emotional from neutral expressions and gazed at eyes least—indicators of social impairment—had a smaller than normal amygdala, an almond-shaped danger-detector deep in the brain. The researchers also linked such amygdala shrinkage to impaired nonverbal social behavior in early childhood.

Social Fear Is the Initial Trigger

The new findings suggest that social fear in autism may initially trigger a hyperactive, abnormally enlarged amygdala, which eventually gives way to a toxic adaptation that kills amygdala cells and shrinks the structure, propose Richard Davidson, Ph.D., and colleagues at the University of Wisconsin, who report on their magnetic resonance imaging (MRI) study in the December 2006 *Archives of General Psychiatry.*

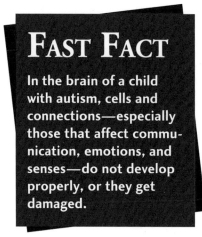

FAST FACT

In the brain of a child with autism, cells and connections—especially those that affect communication, emotions, and senses—do not develop properly, or they get damaged.

In a related study, another research team led by Davidson found that well siblings of people with autism share some of the same differences in amygdala volume, and in the way they look at faces and activate social/emotional brain circuitry, particularly an area critical for face processing.

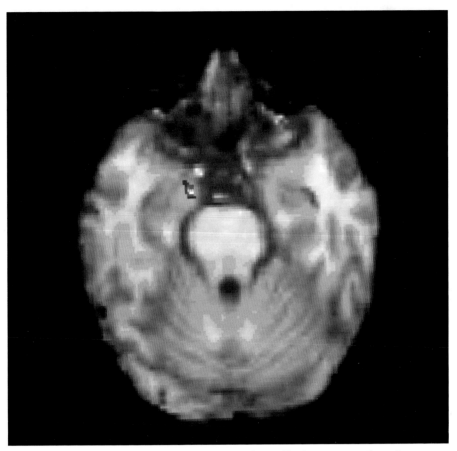

A PET scan shows the left amygdala (highlighted in yellow) reacting to fear. Autism initially triggers a hyperactive, abnormally enlarged amygdala but later leads to an atrophied amygdala.

"Together, these results provide the first evidence linking objective measures of social impairment and amygdala structure and related brain function in autism," explained Davidson. "Finding many of the same differences, albeit more moderate, in well siblings helps to confirm that autism is likely the most severe expression of a broad spectrum of genetically-influenced characteristics."

Avoiding Eye Contact

While some people with minimal expression of these traits might be perceived as aloof or loners, those at the more severe end of the spectrum are unable to engage in give-and-take interactions and fail to develop age-appropriate peer relationships. Notably, they shy away

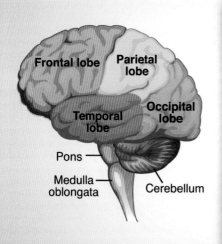

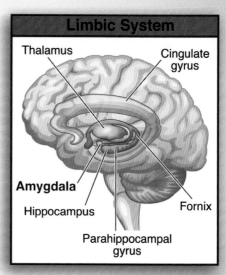

Taken from: American Health Assistance Foundation. www.ahaf.org.

from looking at eyes. Davidson's research team . . . last year [2005] linked such eye-gazing with hyperactivation of their fear hub. Yet different studies have found the amygdala in autism to be variously enlarged, shrunken or even normal in size.

Davidson, Kim Dalton and colleagues suspected that these seemingly inconsistent findings resulted from the wide variability of the autism spectrum, which masked amygdala changes—that a clearer picture would emerge if the length and severity of hypersensitivity to social interactions were factored in. They brought to bear eye-tracking and other measures of facial emotion processing in combination with MRI to find out if degree of non-verbal social impairment might predict amygdala volume in 49 males, aged 8–25, including 25 with autism spectrum disorders.

Unable to Identify Facial Expression

Those in the autism group who had a small amygdala were significantly slower at identifying happy, angry, or sad facial expressions and spent the least time looking at eyes relative to other facial regions. Autistic subjects with the smallest amygdalae took 40 percent longer than those with the largest fear hubs to recognize such emotional facial expressions, and those with the largest amygdalae spent about four times longer looking at eyes than those with the smallest. Eye fixation did not correlate with amygdala volume among 24 control subjects. The size of the amygdala increased early in autism group subjects with normal eye fixation, while it increased little in those with low eye fixation. Moreover, autism group subjects with small amygdalae had the most non-verbal social impairment as children.

Chronic Stress Causes Brain Cell Death

The researchers suggest that the amygdala in autism fits a model in which a brain structure adapts to chronic stress—in this case, fear of people—by first becoming hyperactive, but over time succumbing to a process of toxic cell death and atrophy, as has been proposed occurs in the hippocampus for some forms of depression. Children with autism who are least hypersensitive to interaction with people would thus show slower amygdala shrinkage while those who were most hypersensitive would begin to show amygdala changes early in life. Such amygdala adaptations likely affect most people with autism by adulthood, according to the researchers. However, they caution that these changes do not explain all autistic behavior, but account for slightly more than half of the variability in nonverbal social impairment.

EVALUATING THE AUTHOR'S ARGUMENTS:

After reading this viewpoint, do you think autism causes the brain's "fear hub" to shrink, or that the shrinking of the "fear hub" causes autism? Give reasons for your answer.

ADHD Negatively Affects Adults in Numerous Ways

Steve Bates

"*People with ADHD change jobs more often than other workers and tend to 'gravitate to professions that don't require a lot of sitting time.*'"

In the following viewpoint Steve Bates argues that attention-deficit/hyperactivity disorder (ADHD) causes social, financial, and personal problems for adults who suffer from it. The author cites the results of the Capturing America's Attention study of the disorder. According to the study, adults with ADHD are more likely to have difficulty staying employed. Adults with ADHD, says the author, are also more likely to suffer from depression. However, employers can help employees with ADHD and their company by "sponsoring educational events to raise awareness" about the disorder, which might prompt ADHD-affected employees to seek screening for the disorder, if they have not already. Bates is managing editor of *HR News. HRMagazine* is a monthly magazine of the Society for Human Resource Management.

AS YOU READ, CONSIDER THE FOLLOWING QUESTIONS:
1. How many U.S. adults are potentially affected by ADHD, according to the author?
2. What is the expected loss of U.S. household income per year for someone who suffers from ADHD?
3. How many adults with ADHD are likely to be employed compared to adults without ADHD, according to a survey cited in this viewpoint?

Attention-deficit/hyperactivity disorder (ADHD) affects millions of American workers—many of whom might not be aware of the disorder and how it is affecting their job performance and career potential, according to a major new study of the disorder.

The exact number of adults with ADHD is not known. An estimated 4.3 percent of the U.S. adult population—more than 8 million Americans—is affected by the disorder. Because of the impact of ADHD, the study's authors say, some of these working-age people may be unable to hold a steady job.

The loss of U.S. household income to ADHD symptoms totals nearly $77 billion each year, according to the study, Capturing America's Attention. That equates to at least $8,900 in annual lost income per adult with ADHD. The study, backed by a pharmaceutical company, was presented in May at the American Psychiatric Association annual meeting in Atlanta.

Adults with ADHD may have grown up with the condition and associated impairments, such as reduction in educational and professional achievements, reduced self-image and poor interpersonal relationships, according to the study. It states that 24 percent of adults with ADHD experience symptoms that prevent normal activities, such as work, for an average of 11 days

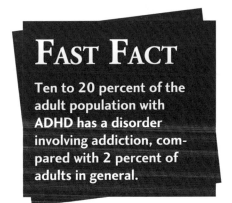

FAST FACT

Ten to 20 percent of the adult population with ADHD has a disorder involving addiction, compared with 2 percent of adults in general.

Adults in Certain Professions Are More Likely Than in Others to Have ADHD

Most Likely

Tradespeople
Entertainers
Elected officials
Health-care workers
Construction workers
Business executives/managers
Clergy, religious workers
Professional and aspiring athletes
Scientists
Teachers
Lawyers
Law enforcement officers
Media professionals
Office, bank, retail store clerks

Least Likely

Taken from: National Institute of Child Health and Development, http://www.nichd.nih.gov.

every month, compared to only 9 percent of adults without the disorder.

Dr. Joseph Biederman, the lead researcher in the ADHD study, said that HR professionals can help affected employees and the organization's bottom line by sponsoring educational events to raise awareness about the underdiagnosed and poorly understood disorder.

HR can sponsor seminars and group discussions of the symptoms and impact of ADHD that might prompt individual employees to seek screening for the disorder on their own, potentially improving their quality of life and workplace productivity, helping the organization in the process, he said.

"Many people don't know they have this. Many people get fired because of this," said Biederman, a professor of psychiatry at Harvard Medical School and chief of pediatric psychopharmacology at Massachusetts General Hospital. "It's characterized by inattention, impulsivity and hyperactivity," he said. "They have trouble with time management, completing tasks, paying attention. They may be late for work, and they are not always prepared."

Not everyone who exhibits these symptoms has ADHD, Biederman noted. But "if the symptoms are persistent, the level of suspicion should go up."

For most people who discover they have ADHD, "it's a great relief to know," Biederman added. They realize that there was a chemical reason for their problems.

Biederman said people with ADHD change jobs more often than other workers and tend to "gravitate to professions that don't require a lot of sitting time." The study found that adults with the disorder

Adults with ADHD are more likely to be unemployed and have a difficult time holding down a job than adults who do not have ADHD.

are three times more likely than others to suffer from stress, depression or other problems with their emotions.

Among other findings:
- Forty-six percent of adults with ADHD indicate a strong tendency toward having a hard time paying attention at work, compared to 20 percent of adults without ADHD.
- Only half of adults with ADHD are employed, compared to 72 percent of adults without the disorder.
- Over the past 10 years, adults with ADHD have had on average 5.4 jobs, compared to 3.4 jobs for people without ADHD.

"The compelling results of this survey reinforce the fact that ADHD is a serious medical condition causing significant, life-long impairments. ADHD can no longer be dismissed as a 'fake' or 'made-up' disorder," Biederman said in announcing the results of the study.

EVALUATING THE AUTHOR'S ARGUMENTS:

The author cites the Capturing America's Attention study to show that adults with ADHD have problems functioning socially, financially, and personally. What evidence does the author give to support the claim that the problems discussed are the result of a real and serious medical condition? Give reasons for your answer.

ADHD Prevents Children from Making Friends

Ascribe Higher Education News Service

"[ADHD] symptoms get in the way of making and keeping friends."

In the following viewpoint, the author argues that children with attention deficit hyperactivity disorder (ADHD) need special training in order to learn to make friends. Problems making friends in childhood, it is argued, results in a spiral of failure as children mature. Friendship skills can be taught to children with ADHD and their parents. Doing so, contends the author, causes marked improvement in overall social skills. Ascribe Higher Education News Service is a public interest wire service.

AS YOU READ, CONSIDER THE FOLLOWING QUESTIONS:

1. According to the author, how many children with ADHD have serious problems making friends?
2. According to the author, how much does ADHD intervention usually focus on developing friendship skills?
3. In addition to making friends more easily, what other positive results have occurred for ADHD children who have participated in "friendship clinic" interventions?

M any children with Attention-Deficit/Hyperactivity Disorder [ADHD] suffer through a range of problems, from poor grades to poor relations with parents and teachers. But more than half of these children also have serious problems making friends. Too often they live lonely lives, never learning to develop the social skills they need to make friends as children or as adults.

Spiral of Failure

"Children with ADHD often are peer-rejected, and their difficulties multiply as they grow to adulthood," said Amori Yee Mikami, assistant professor of psychology at the University of Virginia and principal investigator for a new clinical study designed to help children with ADHD become better at making friends. "Children with ADHD often grow up with depression and relationship problems, some may develop criminal behavior and substance abuse problems," Mikami said. "There can be a spiral of failure that is partly the result of not having learned to make and keep friends as children."

About 5 percent of school-age children are affected by ADHD. Symptoms include a short attention span, poor organization, excessive talking, disruptive and aggressive behavior, restlessness and irritability. Children with ADHD often are uncooperative and may make their own rules.

> **FAST FACT**
>
> The impaired ability of autistic children to imitate others leads to additional impairments in sharing emotions, pretend play, pragmatic communication, and understanding the emotional states of others.

ADHD Symptoms Prevent Friendships

These symptoms get in the way of making and keeping friends," Mikami said. "The child with ADHD can become stigmatized, known as 'the bad kid,' and this can lead to more inappropriate behavior. It can become a vicious cycle resulting in more social isolation."

Treatment for ADHD usually involves medication and counseling designed to help the children improve their attention spans and control impulses. But little intervention is focused on helping children

At "Friendship Clinics" autistic children participate in workshops that help develop social, play, and learning skills as well as friendships with other students.

with ADHD to become better at developing and maintaining good relationships with their peers.

Friendship Skills Can Be Taught

Mikami is working to change that. Through her new "Friendship Clinic," she is developing new methods to help parents help their children with ADHD improve social skills and develop positive behaviors. So far, the results are promising.

Parents and teachers are reporting that the children with ADHD who have participated in the intervention program are making friends more easily, are better behaved, and [are] more willing to cooperate with peers.

"These skills are not easily taught," Mikami said. "Making friends is a proactive process that does not come naturally to children with ADHD. We really have to work closely with the parents and children to set the stage for life-long social skills."

Mikami's clinic offers children with ADHD and their parents an eight-week program involving weekly 90-minute parent group training

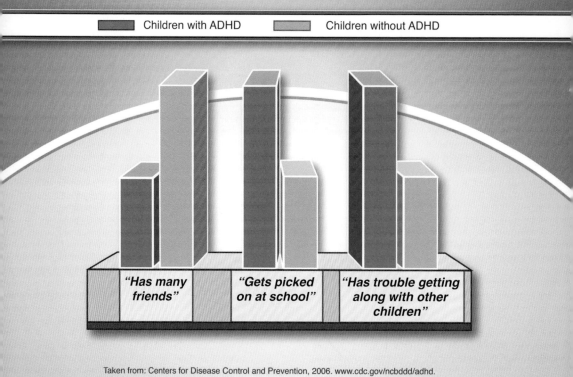

Peer Relationships of Children with ADHD, According to Their Parents

Children with ADHD   Children without ADHD

"Has many friends"

"Gets picked on at school"

"Has trouble getting along with other children"

Taken from: Centers for Disease Control and Prevention, 2006. www.cdc.gov/ncbddd/adhd.

sessions, three one-hour supervised playgroups and "homework" assignments designed to put into practice the techniques learned for making friends. The parents learn new skills as a group working with a therapist, helping each other in the process.

"We teach the parents how to be friendship coaches," Mikami said.

Parents Must Be Taught Also

Parents in the program learn ways to help their children play cooperatively, how to settle social disputes, how to foster a relationship that can last. They learn to help the child pick the right playmate, they learn to structure time for positive activities and to intervene in a positive way when problems develop. Several play dates are arranged to allow Mikami and her colleagues to assess the effectiveness of the training, to see the work in practice.

"We help the parents build a relationship with their child," Mikami said. "We do some role-playing, where the parent steps into the role of the child, to try to understand the world from the child's point of view."

One parent who participated in the treatment group, Stephanie Shelton, said her son Brandon and her entire family have benefited from the program. "I came to know other people who are dealing with the same issues of having a child with ADHD," she said. "It meant we didn't have to deal with this alone. We had a focus group that positively helped us work through issues."

Friendship Training Works

The techniques Shelton learned, such as "active listening," have made her personal time with her son a rich experience. "We look forward to our time together," she said. "And his teacher said she has seen a tenfold improvement in his social skills."

Mikami recently worked with two groups in her study: the "treatment" group, which received training, and a control group of children with ADHD who did not receive training. She is comparing the outcomes of the two groups and is finding that the treatment group children are exhibiting a marked improvement over the ADHD group that did not receive treatment.

The families in the study, from both groups, represent a range of income and education levels and both genders. So far Mikami has worked with 20 families, 10 from each group, and she is planning another phase of the study. "The idea is to help them when they're young, so they may have a lifetime of successful relationships, the kind of positive experiences that will carry over into everything they do," she said.

EVALUATING THE AUTHORS' ARGUMENTS:

After reading this article and the one preceding it, do you believe that ADHD experiences as a child cause the problems that adults with ADHD have functioning in society? Give reasons for your answer.

Chapter 3

How Should Society Address Disabilities Affecting Learning?

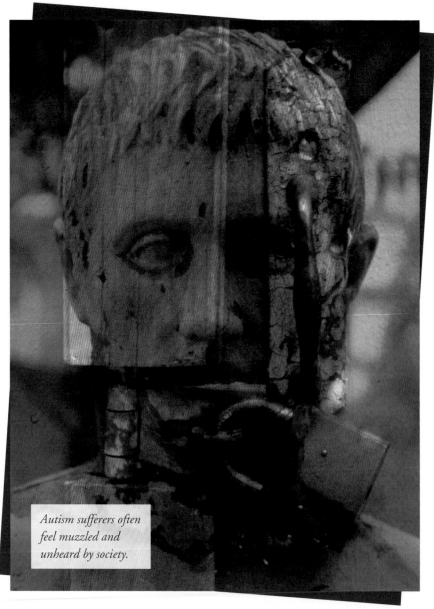

Autism sufferers often feel muzzled and unheard by society.

Viewpoint 1

Special Education Can Help Students with Learning Disabilities

John W. Porter

"For thousands of kids, [laws requiring special education services] give them a shot at a brighter future."

John W. Porter argues in this viewpoint that special education can make a huge difference in the lives of children with learning disabilities. Citing his own experience as a child with a learning disability who received special education, the author argues that providing special education services gives children with learning disabilities a brighter future and also makes them more productive contributors to society. The short-term cost, he contends, is worthwhile in light of the long-term beneficial effect. Porter is senior editor at the *Portland Press Herald* in Maine.

AS YOU READ, CONSIDER THE FOLLOWING QUESTIONS:

1. When was the author diagnosed with a learning disability?
2. In the view of the author, how do local taxpayers often view the cost of special education?
3. What does the author say often determines a parent's ability and willingness to advocate for his or her learning-disabled child?

John W. Porter, "For Kids Who Need It, Special Ed Matters," *Portland Press Herald* (Maine), January 30, 2005. Copyright © 2005 Blethen Maine Newspapers Inc. Reprinted with permission of *Portland Press Herald/Maine Sunday Telegram.*

At the risk of teaching my boy all of my bad study habits, we used our time driving to school on Friday to cram for his spelling test that day.

"I've got an idea," I said. "Why don't you read the words to me and see if I spell them correctly."

"Will that help?"

"Sure," I said. "You'll have to spell them along with me to see that they're right."

So we began to work through the list of words he was having trouble with. They included "irresponsible," "illegal" and my nemesis, "irresistible."

"I-r-r-i-s-i-s-t-i-b-l-e," I said. No, the boy said, that wasn't right. "I-r-r-e!"

More of the rest of the list, then back to the same word. Again I got it wrong. Same mistake. A few minutes later, I did it again a third time.

This is something I live with.

For instance, my son and I have always read together, and when he was younger he especially liked books about dinosaurs. When I'd get

Based on his own personal experience, the author of this viewpoint argues that special education makes a huge difference in the lives of children with learning disabilities.

to one of those dinosaur names with the pronunciation guide next to it, I'd stop cold. I mean, it was like my brain was missing the piece used to process that information. Sometimes 30 seconds would go by before I could take a stab at the unfamiliar word.

Learning Disabilities Can Be Addressed with Special Education

I've covered it up and driven it so deep into my past that I often forget about it. I forget how much it defined me, humiliated me and angered me. I forget how lucky I was that someone saw it for what it was in 1967. I forget how different my life would be had I not come to terms with it.

I have a learning disability.

I want to share this for a couple of reasons. First, to all the students out there who have been labeled "special education" and feel like they can't get any traction, know that it can be done. You can learn to compensate. My particular learning issues—which were not as neatly defined as is often the case now—made it difficult for me to write. I'm talking really difficult here, repeat-the-third-grade difficult. Not just handwriting, which was a struggle, but English composition. When I was in the 6th grade my writing was not anywhere near what my peers could do.

Now consider this: For the past 23 years every dollar I've made has been earned as a writer or editor, and these days, as a senior editor at the state's [Maine] largest newspaper, I'm doing just fine, thank you very much.

Special Ed Is Often Viewed as an Unfair Burden

The more important message, though, has to go out to parents, teachers and especially politicians and the voters. Too often, particularly at the local level, special education is viewed as an unfair burden to the taxpayers. The cliched image is of a kid who has profound issues—the kind that might cost hundreds of thousands of dollars annually to address—in a small district where taxpayers can feel the burden directly.

Throughout government there is a fair amount of buck-passing when it comes to special education. The local towns and cities want the state to pay for it. The state complains that the federal government isn't doing its part. The feds always end up coming up short on it.

Fortunately, there are laws that require that the services be provided, and for thousands of kids across Maine those laws give them a shot at a brighter future. The system for identifying and serving special needs kids is imperfect, however. And as the state tries to address those issues, it's not clear that the remedies being discussed are going to make it better.

Schools Resist Special Education

The system used for identifying kids with special needs is squishy. That's a good thing in some ways, because kids can't be neatly categorized. But it also creates a gross inequity amplified by class. The reality is that, given the costs and the political currents that special ed can generate, school systems sometimes resist classifying kids as special needs. The further reality is that, when a parent knows the law and can be an effective advocate, he or she can usually force the district to provide services.

The unfortunate thing is that a parent's ability and willingness to advocate for his or her child is often determined by that parent's socio-economic status.

FAST FACT

According to U.S. Department of Education estimates, nearly 6 million of the nation's schoolchildren, ages six to twenty-one, receive special education services.

Availability of Services Is Not Equal

The other inequity plays out district to district. Because of differences in local tax bases, the school aid formulas and political support for the education budget, there are big disparities in Maine district-to-district when it comes to special ed.

State Sen. Michael Brennan, D-Portland, says that, in some districts, as few as 7 percent of the kids receive specialized instruction to address a learning disability. In other districts, 35 percent of the kids are considered to have a learning disability.

The school funding law passed by voters last June calls on the state to pay 100 percent of the cost of special education. The devilish

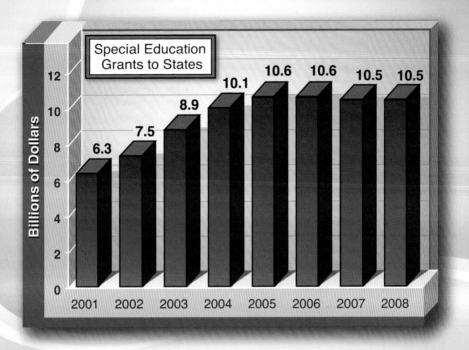

Federal Funding for Special Education

Special Education Grants to States

Billions of Dollars

2001	2002	2003	2004	2005	2006	2007	2008
6.3	7.5	8.9	10.1	10.6	10.6	10.5	10.5

Taken from: Taken from: U.S. Department of Education, www.ed.gov.

details of that policy, though, could make it tougher for some kids to get services while in other cases services could be given out needlessly.

Susan Gendron, the state commissioner of education, says that the first 15 percent of a district's kids who are classified as special ed will bring aid to the district at more than double the rate normally provided on a per-pupil basis. After 15 percent, a little bit more money is given when a kid is classified as special ed, but not anything close to double.

The state is also trying to standardize the criteria used to determine if a kid has a learning disability, Gendron said.

Limiting Spending Will Cost More in the Future

So, in districts where more than 15 percent of the kids are designated as special education, there will be strong incentives to get kids out of those programs. Where fewer than 15 percent are classified as having a learning disability, there will be strong incentives to get more kids into these programs.

I get why state policy makers would want to put some controls on this spending, but maybe that's not terribly smart in the long run. Numerical targets for special education services might serve the bean counters and policy wonks, but do they serve every child?

I'm not a neutral observer here, but from where I sit, it's better that we identify too many kids as special needs than too few. Senior editors at newspapers, after all, make and spend a lot more money—and pay a lot more taxes—than high school dropouts.

EVALUATING THE AUTHOR'S ARGUMENTS:

If special education is as important as the author of this viewpoint contends, how would you determine how much should be spent on special education? How does your view compare with that of the author?

Special Education Is Too Costly

Jennifer Mann

"Special education . . . is squeezing school budgets like never before."

In the following viewpoint, Jennifer Mann asserts that special education is too costly. The federal mandate to provide special education, she says, flooded local schools with disabled children but failed to provide adequate funding for special education. As a result, she says, local schools must cut services for the majority of children who do not need special education, creating friction between parents. Mann writes for the *Patriot Ledger*, located in Quincy, Massachusetts.

AS YOU READ, CONSIDER THE FOLLOWING QUESTIONS:

1. According to the author, how many children in Massachusetts receive at least some special education?
2. How much can special education for a child placed in a private school cost per year, according to figures cited by the author?
3. What percentage does the federal government contribute toward special education on average, according to the author?

R andolph [Massachusetts] eliminated school buses. Scituate delayed opening a much-needed elementary school. Fees could not save Milton from slashing 20 teachers and aides. Yet none of these communities touched special education spending. They can't. It's the law.

Special education, a state- and federally mandated program with a hefty price tag, is squeezing school budgets like never before. Massachusetts spent $1.8 billion on 163,396 special needs students last year. It costs twice as much to educate a special ed student in the state, which is seventh-highest in the nation for special ed enrollment.

Public Money Paying for Private Schools

More public school money is being used to pay for fewer students to attend costly private and specialty schools. Massachusetts is sixth-highest in the nation for the percentage of special ed spending on private and specialty schools at local schools' expense.

Last year, one-third of public school spending on special ed was used to pay private and specialty schools. In some South Shore communities, it accounted for up to half of special ed spending.

A *Patriot Ledger* review of public school spending shows those that spend the most for private and specialty schools placement often spend a disproportionate share of the school budget on special ed.

Regular Ed Versus Special Ed Parents

The high costs are creating worry for school officials and, in some towns, friction between special ed parents and those who say general education is being shortchanged.

"It's regular ed parents against special ed parents," said Marynell Henry, co-chairwoman of a Scituate foundation that supports special ed programs. "It's real easy . . . it's special ed costs, and it may very well be, but . . . we're all a community and we're here to educate and support all our children."

School superintendents fear that spending more money on fewer high need special ed students leaves less for in-house programs that would help all special and regular ed students achieve, said Tom Scott, president of the Massachusetts Association of School Superintendents.

Spending on Special Education in Several Massachusetts Towns

Town	Total budget (millions)	Special education budget	Percent of spending
Halifax	$5.9	$1,786,613	30%
Kingston	$9.7	$2,576,671	27%
Holbrook	$12.0	$3,138,100	26%
Braintree	$44.5	$11,395,243	26%
Randolph	$33.5	$8,322,764	25%
Southeastern	$15.9	$590,881	4%
Silver Lake	$16.4	$819,181	5%
Blue Hills	$12.2	$619,755	5%
Norfolk County	$3.6	$207,363	6%
Old Colony	$5.9	$397,494	7%
South Shore	$6.4	$491,349	7%

Taken from: U.S. Department of Education, www.ed.gov.

"You're not going to hear that as a vocal debate; you're going to hear that as a subtle debate," he said.

There is evidence that their concerns are justified.

Special Ed Is Not Working

In 2005, more than half of Massachusetts school districts failed to meet state standards for special ed students on the English portion of MCAS [Massachusetts Comprehensive Assessment System]. More than 60 percent did not measure up in math, even though advocates say with assistance most special ed students can succeed.

Special ed students in the state also have higher drop-out and in-school violence rates than their peers.

"I understand completely the horrendous financial pressures that are on our districts," said Ellen Chambers, founder of SpEdWatch, an advocacy group. "But the answer to that problem cannot be to deny the proper education to these students."

Schools Were Flooded with Disabled Students

Until the early 1970s, students with severe mental or physical handicaps were placed in private institutions at a parent's expense or in a state-run school. All that changed in 1975 when Congress passed the Education of All Handicapped Children Act, which required a free and appropriate public education for all handicapped students in the least restrictive environment.

Suddenly, teachers had to teach students who used to be in segregated classrooms, and public schools were flooded with severely disabled students as institutions closed or changed their focus.

Today, one in six children in Massachusetts receives at least some special education, and a growing number are diagnosed with disabilities such as autism, rarely seen 30 years ago. Public schools must teach them or pay to send them elsewhere.

Financial Toll on Public Schools

"Given that rise—and given that we identify these children at age 3 and generally have to provide services to that child in a very significant way—it puts a large strain on the school district," said Dover Sherborn Superintendent Perry Davis, co-author of a 2001 report by the Massachusetts Association of School Superintendents on why special ed spending has gone up.

When a public school must pay to place a child in a private school, the yearly toll can be upwards of $100,000 for one child. This can lead to finger-pointing. "I've heard it said: We have a new family in town and now we have to find $50,000—as if that child isn't a human being, but a $50,000 problem," said Earl Fay, the father of two autistic children in Milton public schools.

Federal Government Is Not Helping Enough

In 1975, Congress set a goal of contributing 40 percent to the cost of educating special needs children, but today the federal contribution is closer to 17 percent, varying by state. Massachusetts Sen. Edward Kennedy, a co-sponsor of the law, said the federal government has failed to live up to its commitment to special ed funding.

The $1.8 billion cost in Massachusetts is largely paid by cities and towns, which are limited by state law in their ability to raise new taxes. The state kicks in about 35 percent—not far from the share it pays for regular ed. The federal government kicks in about $400 million for specific grant programs for special ed students.

Barbara Anderson, executive director of Citizens for Limited Taxation, said state or federal human services agencies should be picking up more of the tab. "There's no reason that property taxes should be paying for a human services problem," she said.

FAST FACT

California school districts shift more than a billion dollars a year out of their regular school budgets to pay for special education.

The state's contribution is based on estimates of how much it costs to educate a special ed student, but superintendents say this guess is chronically too low. Further, they say, an emergency state fund to help public schools cope with extraordinary spending for a high needs child falls short because it does not cover transportation costs.

Locals Must Cut Other Services to Pay for Special Ed

The federal No Child Left Behind Act of 2001 holds special ed students to the same standards as general population, but advocates say the mandate has been under-funded. This all leads to a squeeze on the local level.

In Weymouth and Sharon, special ed accounts for nearly a fourth of school budgets, up from 18 percent a decade ago. More than a fourth of Holbrook's school budget goes to special ed, and in Halifax, it is a third.

In Randolph this year [2007], special ed consumed one-third of the district's spending, with a $2 million increase resulting in cuts in other services including sports. "We're required by law to provide those special education services; we're not required by law to provide (busing and sports)," Randolph Superintendent Richard Silverman said.

Inclusion Is Not Working

Superintendents say the goal is for public schools to create in-house or collaborative programs so they spend less on private and specialty schools. The savings would allow schools to devote more resources to early intervention and classroom support so that special and regular ed kids could be taught side by side—what educators call mainstreaming or inclusion.

Advocates say only about a third of the state's 389 public school districts have successfully implemented inclusion. "A lot of school systems say they're doing inclusion, but what they're really doing is just putting kids in the regular classroom without the support, and that's just disastrous," said Kevin Lenane, a special ed administrator in Newton, a district known for its mainstreaming program.

A teacher works with autistic children in a Los Angeles school. Critics say that the federal mandate to provide special education for learning-disabled students has forced schools to cut services to the majority of students.

The result can be battles between special ed parents and administrators over out-of-district placement. "The only time (administrators) start talking about out-of-district is after the kids are falling flat on their face," said Suzanne Gervais, president of the Massachusetts Association of Special Education Parent Advisory Councils.

EVALUATING THE AUTHORS' ARGUMENTS:

After reading this viewpoint and the preceding one, how would you balance the need for special education with the cost of providing it?

Viewpoint

3

ADHD Drugs
Can Help
Many Children

"For many children who have ADHD and need help desperately, the drugs [such as Ritalin] are a breakthrough."

Darshak Sanghavi

Darshak Sanghavi asserts in this viewpoint that Ritalin and similar drugs can provide important help to persons with attention deficit hyperactivity disorder (ADHD). People who suffer from ADHD, he explains, have impaired ability to regulate their thoughts, resulting in a lack of impulse control. He argues that Ritalin can cause immediate and often dramatic improvement in behavior. The popular impression that Ritalin is over-prescribed or dangerous is not well supported by research, he contends. Sanghavi is a pediatric cardiologist at the University of Massachusetts Medical School.

AS YOU READ, CONSIDER THE FOLLOWING QUESTIONS:
1. How many hyperactive behaviors must children display to be diagnosed with ADHD, according to the author?
2. How many doctors use the right questionnaires to diagnose ADHD, according to Sanghavi?
3. According to studies cited by the author, what percentage of children may have ADHD and thus benefit from treatment with drugs like Ritalin?

Today, almost one in 20 children is diagnosed with attention deficit/hyperactivity disorder, or ADHD.

It isn't a condition like strep throat or pneumonia, which a doctor can confirm or refute using a blood test, stethoscope, or brain scan. Like many other psychological problems, ADHD appears to some critics to be a made-up problem that "medicalizes" normal behavior. But, in fact, the increased diagnosis and treatment of ADHD may be a major public health success story.

Inability to Regulate Thoughts

Just as an air-traffic controller supervises the taking off and landing of flights from the runway, the brain's "executive center" coordinates the entry and exit of thoughts from consciousness. To prevent chaos, a controller must decide which flights are urgent, and which may wait.

In ADHD, the air-traffic controller of the mind fails. Thoughts arrive and take off with no regulation. A child may steal something from a classmate without asking. He or she may repeatedly lack impulse control. The condition has serious consequences. Compared with normal children, those with ADHD later get arrested four times more frequently, develop alcoholism and drug problems more often, and end up with lower-paying jobs.

Understanding how doctors think about ADHD explains why so many children have been treated with Ritalin or Adderall and why that may not be so bad despite media attention to "overtreatment."

The Origin of ADHD

The story begins with Charles Bradley, a Rhode Island psychiatrist who in 1937 gave amphetamines to 30 children who were having various problems in school. According to Bradley, 14 children had a "great increase of interest in school material." However, he lacked a reliable system to classify patients. It was like having chemotherapy but no way to tell which children had cancer.

It was not until 1979 that a psychologist named Robert Spitzer essentially made up a disorder he called "attention-deficit disorder," (previously called, among other names, "minimal brain dysfunction" and "hyperkinesis"). He created a list of specific symptoms to make the diagnosis in children.

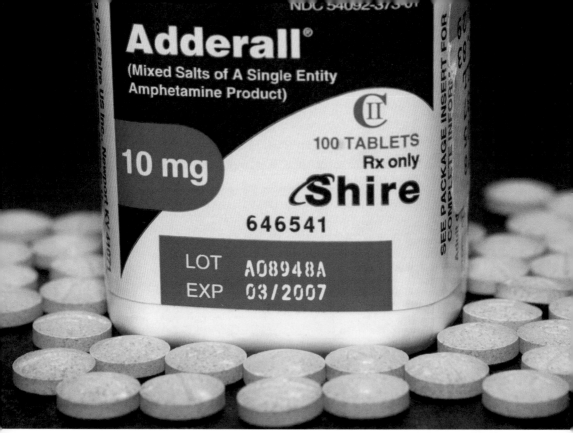

The drug Adderall has been found to be effective in treating ADHD but also controversial because of possible negative side effects.

Medications Work

These weren't just rambunctious kids. Diagnosed children must have at least six hyperactive behaviors such as the inability to sit still, excessive talking, and acting "as if driven by a motor," the onset of symptoms before 7 years of age, impairment of normal school function, and problems at both home and school. Once the diagnosis was more consistent, treatment could be tested scientifically. By 1997, it became clear that affected children responded spectacularly to drug treatment. Researchers at McMaster University in Canada systematically compiled 92 studies and showed that more than 70 percent of patients taking methylphenidate (Ritalin) and dextroamphetamine (Adderall) responded to the drugs.

According to an article in the *New England Journal of Medicine* in 1999, the drugs cause "immediate and often dramatic improvement in behavior. Attentiveness improves, and interpersonal interactions [are] less confrontational."

Side Effects Are Uncertain

Of course, there are many limitations. Studies suggest the drugs slow a child's growth, in part because some children lose their appetite.

Though Canada recently pulled the extended release form of Adderall from shelves for possibly causing a rare cardiac side effect, US regulators found the connection unlikely and didn't follow suit.

And good, controlled trials of the drugs have only followed children for a few years. No one knows for sure if the drugs will really result in long-term academic improvement and reduce high-risk behaviors as children enter adulthood. And taking the drugs for many years may cause unforeseen side effects.

Furthermore, less than two-thirds of doctors use the right questionnaires to diagnose ADHD, perhaps causing misdiagnosis. Some don't check for other problems like depression, which may be an additional or alternative explanation for school problems.

ADHD Drugs Are a Breakthrough

But for many children who have ADHD and need help desperately, the drugs are a breakthrough. Studies estimate that 6 to 11 percent of all children may have ADHD, and thus may benefit from treatment.

Due to increased awareness and diagnosis, drug treatment for ADHD has been skyrocketing. Maryland, which tracks ADHD cases, saw a sixfold increase in diagnoses since the 1970s.

Despite the popular impression that these drugs are overprescribed, no studies in respected medical journals confirm that fear.

> **FAST FACT**
>
> Worldwide, about 75 percent of Ritalin prescriptions are for children, with four times as many boys taking the drug.

Still, some critics think increased diagnosis of ADHD is society's fault. In his book "Ritalin Nation," Richard DeGrandpre blames the uptick in diagnoses on our "rapid-fire culture." Blaming the "authority of American psychiatry," DeGrandpre assails modern culture for allowing kids to become "addicted" to sensory stimulation and encourages parents to slow their own lives and spend time with their kids.

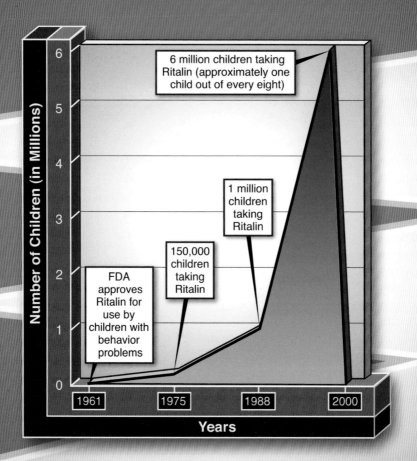

Ritalin Use Is on the Rise in America

Number of Children (in Millions)

6 million children taking Ritalin (approximately one child out of every eight)

1 million children taking Ritalin

150,000 children taking Ritalin

FDA approves Ritalin for use by children with behavior problems

1961 1975 1988 2000

Years

Taken from: "Michigan Ranks Third in U.S. Ritalin Use," *Education Report*, January 10, 2001. www.educationreport.org.

This is a noble idea, but has a curious blame-the-parents subtext that doesn't jive with the data.

ADHD Drugs Are More Effective than Therapy

While behavioral therapy and greater adult involvement have great appeal for treating ADHD, they're less effective than drugs. In a major 1999 National Institute of Mental Health-sponsored project, children getting 35 behavioral therapy sessions, an in-class teaching aide, a summer treatment program, and specialized teacher and parent counseling didn't do much better than another group of children who didn't get such intensive therapy. But a third group on medication did much better, and adding behavioral interventions for children taking the drugs provided some modest benefit.

In the end, we should stop blaming parents, teachers, and pediatricians for diagnosing ADHD. As Malcolm Gladwell writes in *The New Yorker*, the world mourned by critics like DeGrandpre was "a ruthlessly Darwinian place" where kids with "neurological quirks" were simply allowed to fail.

Today, many people are no longer content to see these children left behind and they shouldn't feel guilty for using medicine to help them.

EVALUATING THE AUTHOR'S ARGUMENTS:

Why does the author believe that increased diagnosis of ADHD is a success story rather than a problem?

ADHD Drugs Are Overprescribed and Harmful to Children

"[Drugs] are being massively over-prescribed to some children that are simply naughty."

Barbara Davies

In the following viewpoint Barbara Davies argues that Ritalin and other powerful drugs are being overprescribed to children. These drugs have dangerous side effects, she contends, and are given in large dosages that worsen rather than improve the child's condition. Drug companies are promoting such drugs, she says, because they are profitable. Davies writes for the *Daily Mail* in London, England.

AS YOU READ, CONSIDER THE FOLLOWING QUESTIONS:

1. According to the author, how many deaths among children and adults taking Ritalin have occurred in the United States since 1999?
2. According to an expert quoted by the author, why are children who are prescribed Ratalin at high risk for later use of street drugs?
3. According to a study on the long-term effects of Ritalin cited by the author, how long did it take for the effects of Ritalin to wear off?

W hen he was in the throes of his worst tantrums, Daniel Fletcher would rip wallpaper off the walls at home and hit and kick anyone who came near him. Once, he put his pet mouse in the microwave. On another occasion he jumped out of a moving car.

Ritalin Did Not Help

He was first diagnosed with Attention-Deficit Hyperactivity Disorder (ADHD) at the age of two, and just three years later the little boy was prescribed the amphetamine-like drug Ritalin. The effect, says his mother Hayley, was a loss of appetite but no difference in his behaviour.

'So the doctor kept upping the doses until he was on six times the normal dose, yet he was still hyperactive.' Eight months ago, Daniel, now 14, was put on Risperdal—an antipsychotic drug usually given to schizophrenics. 'It was as if my son had been replaced by a doped-up zombie,' says Hayley, 35, who took him off it a month later. 'I could hardly wake him in the morning. It was as if all his personality was disappearing, like a patient in a mental institution.' Last week [November 2007], it emerged that around 8,000 British youngsters are being treated with this powerful tranquilliser and another, similar drug called Zyprexa—despite the fact that their dangerous side-effects range from diabetes to brain tumours.

Dangerous Side Effects

Hundreds of thousands of others are still being prescribed Ritalin, an amphetamine-like stimulant which has the same effect as 'speed' and cocaine, and which, according to new evidence from the U.S., doesn't even work in the long-term.

Ritalin is a methylphenidate which acts in a similar way to cocaine by stimulating the central nervous system, which, paradoxically, can have a calming and focusing effect.

Scientists are unclear why it works in this way, although there is some evidence that the effect is achieved by the slow release of the hormone dopamine, which controls behaviour, attention and learning.

Recent findings also suggest that Ritalin can stunt growth as well as cause heart problems, insomnia and weight problems.

In the U.S., there have been 51 deaths among children and adults taking Ritalin since 1999. According to the Medicines and Healthcare Products Regulatory Agency, 11 British children on Ritalin have died.

The cause of two deaths was heart related: one had a heart attack, the other an enlarged heart. One was recorded as a 'sudden death'. One died of a brain haemorrhage; another of a swelling in the brain. Two committed suicide, and the last died of neo-natal respiratory distress syndrome.

Some Children Are Just Naughty, Not Sick

Not surprisingly, experts fear that inappropriate drugs are not only being used to control children's behaviour, but are being massively over-prescribed to some children who are simply naughty. ADHD, they say, is nothing more than a symptom of Britain's time-poor society, where children of parents working long hours are cracking under the strain of family life.

There are criticisms, too, that some doctors dole out pills when therapy would be a safer option. In the U.S., where one in ten children takes Ritalin and where doctors write two million prescriptions a month, the situation is even worse. A growing body of experts is even questioning whether ADHD exists at all. 'As a society, we are quick to reach for a pill,' says David Healy, one of the world's leading psycho-pharmacology experts, and Professor of Psychiatry at Cardiff University.

'There's much less willingness on the part of the medical profession to say to parents: "You have an awkward child. You must discipline them." So we prescribe pills instead.

Overprescribing Powerful Drugs

'The drugs used to treat ADHD are the same as speed and cocaine. We react with horror to the idea that our kids would use such drugs, but don't react about drugs such as Ritalin being given to them.

'There's a risk that your child won't grow as well. There are high risks that children will go on to use street drugs, too, because they will have grown used to their effects.' Professor Healy says anti-psychotic drugs such as Risperdal were used in the Soviet Union to extract information from political prisoners.

A pharmacist holds a bottle of the ADHD drug Ritalin and a pamphlet that warns parents about the drug's potential to be abused by teenagers.

'People who took them would tell anything to anyone,' he says. 'When you think about giving these drugs to kids, it's a whole new ball game.' Dr Tim Kendall of the Royal College of Psychiatrists, who is heading a team drawing up new NHS [National Health Service, Britain's universal health care service] guidelines for ADHD, insists there is a place for drugs in treatment, but admits: 'We have a situation where GPs [general practitioners] prescribe anti-psychotics inappropriately.

'There is no real excuse for prescribing drugs which are associated with such severe side-effects.' But even where Ritalin is used, Dr Kendall says guidelines do not make it clear when doctors should diagnose ADHD and when they should prescribe drugs. 'If you diagnose people loosely, you could end up with 16 per cent of the child population with ADHD. Under tight criteria, only 1.6 per cent would be diagnosed,' he says.

'A generous understanding would be to say that doctors have reached a point where they don't know what else to offer, and they haven't got the right support to help parents.' Of course, the ADHD debate inevitably arouses enormous passions. While some question the disorder's very existence and say, medicating has simply replaced good parenting, for others, the idea that 'bad parenting' is behind their child's problems is almost too much to bear.

Some Say the Benefit Outweighs the Danger

Linda Shepherd, from Ipswich, whose son Zaque, 15, has been taking Risperdal, since he was nine, describes the drug as a 'life-saver'. 'Without it, he's unmanageable,' she says. 'It controls his ADHD and gives us both peace of mind.

'I know there are side-effects, but for me it's a calculated risk. He's put on a lot of weight and is now obese because the drug makes him hungry all the time, but I think that's the lesser of two evils.' A spokeswoman for ADDISS, the Attention Deficit Disorder Information & Support Service, which believes medication has a valuable role to play, says: 'Every child needs a proper evaluation and a treatment programme tailored to their problem.

'It's not one issue. It's a collection of factors. The problem is that people don't have access to comprehensive evaluation and treatment. But not giving them medication is worse.' Although there is no consensus on what ADHD is and, if it exists, what causes it, there is no doubt it has become a fashionable diagnosis for a host of behavioural issues.

No Long-Term Benefits

In 1993, just 3,500 prescriptions were written for Ritalin in Britain. By 1998, there were 26,500. Last year, around 250,000 prescriptions were handed out on the NHS alone. Such figures are underpinned by a study in 1999, which appeared to confirm Ritalin's benefits.

But eight years on, the original researchers have re-examined the children involved in the study and there is evidence the initial effects of Ritalin wore off after three years.

Ritalin was also found to stunt the growth of some of the children. Professor William Pelham, of the University of Buffalo, New York, who was involved in the first study, says: 'They had a substantial decrease in their rate of growth in terms of both height and weight.

'In the short-term, medication will help the child behave better. But in the long run it won't. And that information should be made very clear to parents.'

Drug Companies Are Pushing ADHD Drugs

Perhaps most disturbing, however, is the suggestion that ADHD is nothing more than the invention of pharmaceutical companies who have used clinical trials to create a disease that can be treated with their drugs. Last year, the NHS spent [pounds sterling] 28 million on Ritalin alone.

Professor Healy says: 'There is an active campaign by pharmaceutical companies to convince people that there's adult ADHD. Adults having problems are being told they have adult ADHD and are being offered drugs for it.

'Pharmaceutical companies market these drugs aggressively. How can GPs refuse to prescribe a drug 'clinically proven' to work?' It is hardly surprising, then, that parents encouraged to give drugs to their children, rather than face up to the causes of their behaviour, usually take the easy way out.

> **FAST FACT**
>
> In one study that looked at adult cocaine users, it was found that those individuals who used Ritalin between one and ten years of age had a percentage of cocaine abuse twice that of those who had been diagnosed with ADHD but had not taken Ritalin.

Excessive Dosages

Hayley Fletcher, who lives with her husband Andrew and their son Daniel in King's Lynn, Norfolk, remembers the moment her son's psychiatrist handed her a prescription for Risperdal.

'You assume the experts know best,' she says. 'But within a month, I knew something was terribly wrong. I couldn't wake him in the mornings. It was as if my son was disappearing before my eyes.

I did some research and found they give this brain-altering drug to adults in mental institutions.

'Why did they give it to my son? He has severe problems, there is no doubt about that, but I cannot agree with the philosophy that these children should be drugged up to the eyeballs so they cannot be a threat to society. That isn't what I want for my son.' Instead, Hayley persuaded Daniel's doctor to change his medication to the weaker drug Concerta, a slow-release version of Ritalin, and improved his diet with natural produce and fish oils. She also removed him from his special school and teaches him at home.

'It's been a very long, hard path,' she says, 'but Daniel is a different boy. The difference is amazing.

'Initially, I trusted the doctors. But really all they are doing is turning these children into zombies.' Her son's story echoes that of Craig Buxton, 14. . . .

Drugs Can Make ADHD Worse

Craig, who lives with his parents, Alan and Sharon, in Stoke-on-Trent, was given both Risperdal and Zyprexa. 'The effects were dramatic and awful,' says Sharon. 'Within a month, he had started self-harming, cutting himself. Then he attempted suicide by cutting his wrist.

'He's taking Concerta now, and is much more stable and happy.' John Tyson, 39, a businessman from Yarm, Teesside, didn't question the paediatrician who put his 'restless, bouncy, fidgety' son John, now 15, on Ritalin two years ago.

'When it's a doctor you just smile and nod,' he says. 'I knew nothing about the drug or how toxic it was. But things rapidly went downhill once John started taking it.

'He became aggressive and he couldn't cope with the word "no". He became a horrible person. The doctors increased the dose and he turned into a monster. He was headbutting walls and throwing things out of the window. The doctors said: "You need more Ritalin."' Eventually, Mr Tyson turned for help to the Cactus Clinic at the University of Teeside's school of social sciences. The groundbreaking centre uses a drug-free approach, and helps children learn appropriate behaviour. The clinic also refuses to use the term ADHD.

Alternatives to Drugs

'Attention disorders are not diseases, but patterns of inappropriate behaviour,' says clinic manager Amanda Clarkson.

According to Mr Tyson, who cut gluten, wheat and dairy out of his son's diet and gave him mineral supplements: 'After six weeks, the benefits were noticeable. After three months, I knew I was getting my boy back. I think it's wicked how children are being doped when there are alternatives.' The treatment, however, is not free.

Parents can pay up to [pounds sterling] 600. Money well spent, according to Mr Tyson, but he says it should be available to all on the NHS.

For the time being, however, it seems the medical consensus is that drugs do have a place in controlling children's behaviour, although next year could see dramatic changes.

Guidelines to Reduce Overprescription

NHS guidelines on ADHD and its treatment are being revised after concerns were raised that current treatment is not consistent.

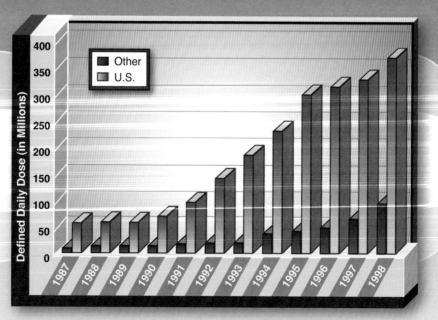

Taken from: Terrance Woodworth, Deputy Director of the Drug Enforcement Administration, Congressional Testimony, May 16, 2000. www.usdoj.gov/dea.

The National Institute for Health and Clinical Excellence has spent two years investigating the disorder and its treatment and will deliver its preliminary findings in January. Experts led by Dr Tim Kendall are looking at the criteria under which ADHD should be diagnosed and, if it exists, the best treatment.

Most likely, the guidelines will be aimed at reducing the over-prescription of drugs, while recognising their usefulness in extreme cases. 'We are looking at dietary interventions,' says Dr Kendall. 'There is some evidence that coal tar derivatives found in things such as diet colas increase hyperactivity.

'There is some evidence that fish oils improve things. There is evidence that education can help teachers deal better with hyperactive children, and that parent training programmes are helpful.' The final NICE guidelines are not likely to be released until next summer. Until then, the only winners are the pharmaceutical companies.

Drug Companies Defend Drugs

According to a spokesman for Janssen-Cilag, maker of Risperdal: 'We don't recommend the use of Risperdal for children. Doctors are free to prescribe the drugs they feel are most appropriate.' Eli Lilly, U.S.-based maker of Zyprexa, says it has never promoted its use for ADHD. And Novartis, which makes Ritalin, says: 'Ritalin has a long record as a safe and effective medication. It is important that medication is only one part of a total treatment programme that should include psychological social and educational measures.' For parents and children still baffled by the ADHD debate, such words bring little comfort.

'I'm not sure my son ever had anything called ADHD,' says John Tyson. 'He just needed a bit of help. He didn't need to be doped.'

EVALUATING THE AUTHORS' ARGUMENTS:

After reading this article and the one preceding it, do you think the way drugs such as Ritalin are used today should be changed? What would you change, and why?

Viewpoint 5

Preventing Exposure to Toxins Could Reduce Learning Disabilities

Steven Kouris

"Toxic exposures during pregnancy and early childhood [are] a preventable cause of neuro-developmental disabilities in the U.S. and around the world."

Steven Kouris contends in this viewpoint that many developmental disabilities in children could be prevented by reducing environmental toxins. Such toxins, he says, can have serious effects on children, especially if the exposure occurs during a critical stage of development. The harmful effect of many toxins, such as lead and mercury, are well documented, he says, but other less-studied toxins also should be regulated as a precaution. Kouris is a pediatric and developmental neuropsychiatrist. He is an associate professor and the chairman of psychiatry at the University of Illinois College of Medicine at Rockford.

AS YOU READ, CONSIDER THE FOLLOWING QUESTIONS:
1. How does the exposure of children to environmental toxins compare to that of adults, according to the author?
2. According to the author, how much human safety data exists for the vast majority of chemicals to which we are routinely exposed?
3. How does lead affect intellect and learning ability, according to the author?

Toxic exposures during pregnancy and early childhood continue to play an important role as a preventable cause of neurodevelopmental disabilities in the U.S. and around the world. Identifying and eliminating these toxins should be a priority but the task is made exceedingly difficult due to the severe limits of scientific knowledge in this area as well as the competing interests of industry and commerce. . . .

Children More Susceptible to Toxins

From conception through at least the first decade of life, children are recognized to have a heightened susceptibility to environmental insult. Additionally, critical windows of vulnerability exist relative to brain development and proper maturation of the central nervous system. Children's overall exposure to environmental contaminants is also increased compared to adults. Many substances a mother comes in contact with may cross the placental barrier and affect her fetus. After birth, a child still has an incomplete blood-brain barrier, immature metabolic pathways, and disproportionately greater intestinal absorption of nutrients and contaminants. Pound for pound, children take in more air, water and food than adults. Dwelling nearer to the ground with an enlarged surface area, children are exposed to more dust and soil, heavy vapors and any contaminants present on floors and in carpets. And as parents of young children know, everything goes into a child's mouth as well.

Toxins Cause Abnormal Development

Manifestations of abnormal development caused by toxic exposure can range from fetal death and structural birth defects to retarded growth and developmental or behavioral disability. An estimated 12 million children in the U.S. now suffer from one or more developmental disabilities. In some parts of the country, rates of reported autism and other developmental disorders are markedly increased. As mounting concerns for possible environmental factors are publicly expressed, little information has been forthcoming. Surprisingly, there exists no human safety data for the vast majority of chemicals we are routinely exposed to in our environment, and currently, there is no

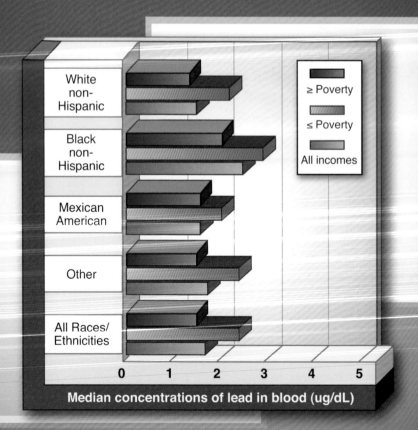

Lead Concentrations in Children

This graph shows median concentrations of lead in the blood of children ages one to five, by race/ethnicity and family income, 2001–2004. The data indicates that poor children and black children have higher concentrations of lead in their blood.

Legend:
- ≥ Poverty
- ≤ Poverty
- All incomes

Categories: White non-Hispanic, Black non-Hispanic, Mexican American, Other, All Races/Ethnicities

Median concentrations of lead in blood (ug/dL)
0   1   2   3   4   5

Taken from: Environmental Protection Agency, "America's Children and the Environment," 2008. www.epa.gov.

nationwide system for collecting toxic exposure data. What is known is restricted to a relatively small number of substances. Extensive data exist on the effects of lead, mercury, alcohol, nicotine and PCB's (polychlorinated biphenyls). Less extensive but substantial data exist for some neurotoxic pesticides and solvents, other than alcohol. There are still fewer data on other compounds such as manganese, fluoride and brominated flame-retardants.

Harm Is Well Documented

Lead is a well-known neurodevelopmental toxin that impairs intellect and learning ability, produces inattention, impulsiveness and hyperactivity, and, more recently, has been causally linked to predatory aggression in animals and juvenile delinquency in humans. As this substance has been removed from paints and fuels, exposure levels have steadily and markedly dropped. Unfortunately, the toxic effects continue to be seen even at very low levels (2.5 ug/dl) of exposure. It appears that perhaps no level of exposure is safe for children after all.

Mercury, likewise, is a well-documented toxin. Effects from high dose exposure during pregnancy include impaired intellect, seizures, visual, auditory and sensory disturbances, cerebral palsy, abnormal movements with problems walking, swallowing and speaking. Low doses impair motor skills, attention, memory, language and visual spatial abilities. As a result, strict limits are advised for fish consumption, especially by pregnant mothers. Coal-fired power plant emissions are also being more closely regulated.

FAST FACT

According to a 2006 study, after the removal of heavy metals that had built up in children's bodies, parents reported improvement in their children's behaviors.

PCB's, a class of chemicals used to insulate electrical transformers, are no longer produced. PCB's persist indefinitely in the environment, however, and bioaccumulate in the food chain. Effects in the exposed infant include reduced birth weight, head circumference, gestational age, and impaired performance on the Brazelton Neonatal Behavioral Assessment in the areas of motor immaturity, emotional ability and startle response. In early childhood, effects may

As part of a national effort to increase monitoring of toxins, a University of Nebraska geologist sets up a mercury monitoring station to track mercury levels in North Platte.

include problems with memory, attention, verbal ability, information processing, psychomotor development and mood regulation. Older children may have diminished intellect, memory, attention and reading comprehension.

More Data Needed for Certain Toxins

The most commonly used brominated flame retardants (PBDE's) resemble PCB's in chemical structure. Exposure to these chemicals during critical windows of brain development decreases memory and learning in animals. No human data exist yet, but these chemicals are now documented to be present in human breast milk in U.S. and Canadian populations.

Organophosphate pesticides cause decreased brain weight, decreased cholinergic receptors, hyperactivity, motor and coordination problems in laboratory animals. Human effects are unknown; however, high rates of human exposure are reported. Among urban newborns, 95% to 100% were exposed. One study found a correlation between umbilical blood levels and head circumference. A CDC study found organophosphate pesticide residues in 75% of the general U.S. population and 90% of children, with the highest concentrations found in the children.

Regulation of Toxins Is Needed

Despite the lack of incontrovertible evidence linking all environmental toxins to specific health outcomes, adoption of a precautionary principle was proposed by [organizers of a conference at the University of Wisconsin called Making the Connection: Human Health and Environmental Exposures]: "When an activity raises the threats of harm to the environment or human health, precautionary measures should be taken, even if some cause and effect relationships are not yet fully established." It remains to be seen whether regulatory authorities will see the wisdom in such an approach.

EVALUATING THE AUTHOR'S ARGUMENTS:

What do you think about the author's argument that toxins that have not been researched should be regulated as a precaution? What arguments can you make for and against doing so?

Viewpoint

6

Schools Should Prepare Learning-Disabled Students for Employment

"We have not used the appropriate instructional methods ... to help [students with learning disabilities] plan for and sustain employment."

D. Richard Johnson, Daryl F. Mellard, and Paula Lancaster

In the following viewpoint D. Richard Johnson, Daryl F. Mellard, and Paula Lancaster assert that schools have failed in their responsibility to prepare learning-disabled (LD) students to function successfully in the workplace. The authors argue that high school graduates with learning disabilities usually try to enter the workforce but fail to obtain and keep employment. They contend that schools must provide LD students with the social skills necessary to succeed at employment. Johnson and Mellard are affiliated with the University of Kansas, and Lancaster is a professor at Grand Valley State University.

U.S. schools expend a great deal of energy preparing children and youth with disabilities "to lead productive and independent adult lives, to the maximum extent possible" in compliance with the Individuals With Disabilities Education Act. Yet, despite supporting federal legislation, research on effective practices, and an emphasis on interagency collaboration, progress in creating effective, comprehensive transition services has been slow.

LD Students Are Ill Prepared by Schools

Clearly, adolescents with learning disabilities (LD) can be difficult to engage in the learning process, and they are often ill-prepared to succeed in high school and beyond. Before exiting school, many of these students evidence performance and adjustment problems, such as higher rates of absenteeism, lower grade-point averages, higher course failure rates, more prevalent feelings of low self-esteem, and higher rates of inappropriate social behaviors than in the general population of students. Those outcomes can lead one to question whether the educational system has used the best methods in teaching these students. Further, one may also wonder: What will these students' success be as they begin participating as adults in the workforce and community?

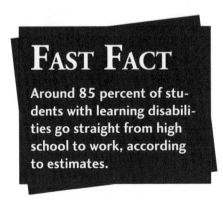

FAST FACT

Around 85 percent of students with learning disabilities go straight from high school to work, according to estimates.

LD Students Are Future Employees

Regardless of their readiness, most young adults with disabilities—over half of whom reported having LD—transitioned into employment within 2 years of leaving school. The recent National Longitudinal Transition Study 2 (NLTS-2) described the experiences of youth (ages 15–19) with disabilities during the first 2 years after exiting from school and found that 75% of this population engaged in post secondary education, job training, or employment. Of those individuals engaged in these three activities, 60% participated solely in employment, 35% were employed and enrolled in post secondary education or job training programs, and 5% were enrolled solely in postsecondary education or job training programs.

A learning-disabled teen receives job training at the Walgreens training center in Anderson, South Carolina. Walgreens plans to train two hundred disabled people for employment.

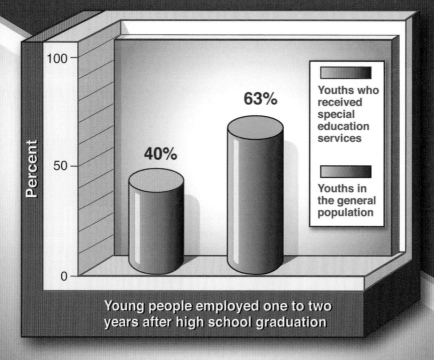

Learning-Disabled Young Adults Struggle with Employment

Percent

100

63%

40%

50

0

Youths who received special education services

Youths in the general population

Young people employed one to two years after high school graduation

Taken from: *San Diego Union-Tribune*, October 13, 2006. www.signonsandiego.com.

LD Workers Do Not Stay Employed

Despite the number of youth with disabilities who enter employment after completing secondary education, the judgment of the National Council on Disability is that "the Department of Education transition initiative has not met with the degree of success expected, hoped and needed." In fact, less than 5% were employed throughout the entire 2-year post-graduation period addressed by the NLTS-2. Moreover, many of the youth reported holding several jobs for only brief periods: 27% of youth with disabilities held a job for 2 months or less, 35% held employment for only 2.1 to 6 months, and only about 8% worked for 12.1 to 24 months. This pattern of brief periods of employment may be due, in part, to the tendency of youth, while still in school, to hold temporary jobs that end shortly thereafter. With regard to individuals with LD, little research exists that investigates their longer-term employment experiences.

LD Students Need Social Skills Instruction

The NLTS-2 data indicated youth with disabilities faced significant barriers and had limited success transitioning to sustained employment. One consistently identified barrier to successful transition for youth with disabilities was poor social skills (i.e., inadequate psychosocial adjustment and problems with interpersonal relationships with peers, teachers, and employers that lead to disciplinary actions at school, being fired from a job, or even being arrested). Furthermore, youth with disabilities infrequently communicated and advocated their own interests and needs. Only 16% of youth with disabilities exhibited high social skills, whereas 22% had markedly low social skills. At a minimum, this 22% of youth with disabilities needed more purposeful instruction, focused content, and practice with the skills required to obtain and sustain employment. The need for such interventions is even more crucial for those students with LD. Some transition experts suggest that learning of social skills, such as community participation, self-determination, communication, and interpersonal relationships, should become a matter of focus and everyday practice.

Schools Must Do More

These figures, together with the problematic nature of preparing youth with disabilities at the secondary level, make it imperative that both educators and adult service providers have appropriate and more effective means to help students with disabilities plan and prepare for employment. As educators, we must ask ourselves whether we have failed this population, particularly because we have not used the appropriate instructional methods nor provided the right content to help them plan for and sustain employment as they enter life after high school.

EVALUATING THE AUTHORS' ARGUMENTS:

Given the difficulty youth with learning disabilities have transitioning to employment, do you believe LD services should be continued beyond high school for youth with LD? Why or why not?

Facts About Disabilities Affecting Learning

Editor's note: These facts can be used in reports or papers to reinforce or add credibility when making important points or claims.

Learning Disabilities in the United States
According to LDHope.com:
- Of special education students identified as learning disabled (LD), 75 to 80 percent have their basic deficits in language and reading.
- Of students identified with learning disabilities, 35 percent drop out of high school.
- About 2.25 million children in public schools have learning disabilities.
- Of adults with severe literacy problems, 60 percent have undetected or untreated learning disabilities.
- Of juvenile delinquents tested, 50 percent were found to have undetected learning disabilities.
- Up to 60 percent of adolescents in treatment for substance abuse have learning disabilities.
- Of learning disabled students, 62 percent were unemployed one year after graduation.
- Of adolescents with learning disabilities, 31 percent will be arrested three to five years out of high school.

According to the Learning Disabilities Association of Washington:
- Nearly 2.9 million students are currently receiving special education services for learning disabilities in the United States.
- Of students receiving special education services through the public schools, 50 percent are identified as having learning disabilities.
- The majority of all individuals with learning disabilities have difficulties in the area of reading.
- Two-thirds of secondary students with learning disabilities are reading three or more grade levels behind and 20 percent are reading five or more grade levels behind.

- Of parents who noticed their child exhibiting signs of difficulty with learning, 44 percent waited a year or more before acknowledging their child might have a serious problem.
- More than 27 percent of children with learning disabilities drop out of high school, compared to 11 percent of the general student population.
- Two-thirds of high school graduates with learning disabilities were rated "not qualified" to enter a four-year college, compared to 37 percent of nondisabled graduates.
- Only 13 percent of students with learning disabilities (compared to 53 percent of students in general population) have attended a four-year post-secondary school program within two years of leaving high school.

Attention Deficit Hyperactivity Disorder (ADHD)
- The *British Medical Journal* estimates that some 7 percent of school-age children have ADHD—and that boys are affected three times as often as girls.
- According to ADHD expert Richard A. Barkley, the symptoms of ADHD on average arise between 3 and 6 years of age, particularly for subtypes of ADHD associated with hyperactive and impulsive behavior. Fifty to 80 percent of children clinically diagnosed with ADHD in childhood will continue to meet the criteria for diagnosis in adolescence.

According to the Centers for Disease Control and Prevention (CDC):
- In 2002, 7 percent of children in the United States ages six to eleven had ADHD.
- Half of children in whom a diagnosis of ADHD was made also have a learning disability. The CDC calculated that at least 1 million children have a learning disability without ADHD. The total number of children with at least one of these disorders was 2.6 million.
- The average annual increase in childhood ADHD diagnoses from 1997 to 2006 was 3 percent, and children with ADHD diagnoses were more likely than other kids to have other chronic health conditions.
- A survey indicated that ADHD is more common among adolescents and teens than among younger kids; more common among whites

or African American children than among Hispanic children; and more common among kids covered by Medicaid than among uninsured or privately insured kids.

Autism

According to the American Society for Autism:

- One in 150 children born has some form of autism.
- Between 1 and 1.5 million Americans have some form of autism.
- Autism is the fastest-growing developmental disability.
- Autism is growing at an annual rate of 10 to 17 percent.
- Autism costs $90 billion annually.
- Of the costs for autism, 90 percent are for adult services.
- Costs of lifelong care for autism can be reduced by two-thirds with early diagnosis and intervention.
- In ten years the estimated annual cost of autism in the United States will be $200–400 billion.

Organizations to Contact

The editors have compiled the following list of organizations concerned with the issues debated in this book. The descriptions are derived from materials provided by the organizations. All have publications or information available for interested readers. The list was compiled on the date of publication of the present volume; the information provided here may change. Be aware that many organizations take several weeks or longer to respond to queries, so allow as much time as possible.

Autism Research Institute
4182 Adams Ave.
San Diego, CA 92116
(866) 366-3361
Web site: http://autism.com

The Autism Research Institute (ARI), a nonprofit organization, was established in 1967. For more than forty years, ARI has devoted its work to conducting research and to disseminating the results of research on the triggers of autism and on methods of diagnosing and treating autism. ARI provides research-based information to parents and professionals around the world. The searchable ARI Web site has extensive information on autism.

Autism Society of America (ASA)
7910 Woodmont Ave., Ste. 300
Bethesda, MD 20814-3067
(301) 657-0881
Web site: www.autism-society.org

ASA, a grassroots autism organization, exists to improve the lives of all affected by autism. ASA attempts to increase public awareness about the day-to-day issues faced by people on the autism spectrum, advocating for appropriate services for individuals of all ages and providing the latest information regarding treatment, education, research, and advocacy. The organization publishes *Autism Advocate,* and the group's Web site has articles and research about autism.

Council for Exceptional Children (CEC)
1110 North Glebe Rd., Ste. 300
Arlington, VA 22201
(703) 620-3660
e-mail: service@cec.sped.org
Web site: www.cec.sped.org

The Council for Exceptional Children (CEC) is an international professional organization dedicated to improving the educational success of individuals with disabilities and/or gifts and talents. CEC advocates for appropriate governmental policies, sets professional standards, provides professional development, advocates for individuals with exceptionalities, and helps professionals obtain conditions and resources necessary for effective professional practice. The organization's Web site has resources concerning the Individuals with Disabilities Education Act.

International Dyslexia Association
40 York Rd., 4th Flr.
Baltimore, MD 21204
(410) 296-0232
Web site: www.interdys.org

The International Dyslexia Association (IDA) is an international organization that concerns itself with the complex issues of dyslexia. The IDA membership consists of a variety of professionals in partnership with dyslexics and their families. The IDA promotes effective teaching approaches and related clinical educational intervention strategies for dyslexics. IDA publishes *Annals of Dyslexia,* an interdisciplinary, peer-reviewed journal dedicated to the scientific study of dyslexia and related language disabilities, and IDA's Web site has informative fact sheets on dyslexia.

Learning Disabilities Association of America (LDA)
4156 Library Rd.
Pittsburgh, PA 15234-1349

(412) 341-1515
Web site: www.ldanatl.org

LDA is a nonprofit volunteer organization advocating for individuals with learning disabilities and has over two hundred state and local affiliates in forty-two states and Puerto Rico. LDA's international membership of over fifteen thousand includes members from twenty-seven countries around the world. The membership, composed of individuals with learning disabilities, family members and concerned professionals, advocates for students with learning disabilities and for adults affected by learning disabilities. The state and local affiliates, through their affiliation with the national LDA, work continuously for individuals with learning disabilities, their parents, and the professionals who serve them. The organization's Web site has informative position papers on issues related to learning disabilities.

National Autism Association
1330 W. Schatz Ln.
Nixa, MO 65714
(877) 622-2884
Web site: www.nationalautismassociation.org/

The mission of the National Autism Association is to educate and empower families affected by autism and other neurological disorders, while advocating on behalf of those who cannot fight for their own rights. The organization's Web site has many articles on autism.

National Center for Learning Disabilities (NCLD)
381 Park Ave. South, Ste. 1401
New York, NY 10016
(212) 545-7510 or toll-free: (888) 575-7373
Web site: www.ncld.org

NCLD provides essential information to parents, professionals, and individuals with learning disabilities; promotes research and programs to foster effective learning; and advocates for policies to protect and strengthen educational rights and opportunities. The organization's searchable database has information about learning disabilities useful both to parents and educators.

National Institute on Early Childhood Development and Education

Office of Educational Research and Improvement
U.S. Department of Education
555 New Jersey Ave. NW
Washington, DC 20208
(202) 219-1935
Web site: www.ed.gov

The National Institute on Early Childhood Development and Education (ECI) was created to carry out a comprehensive program of research, development, and the spread of information to improve early childhood development and learning. The institute helps its customers through its own research as well as through grants for national research and development centers and for field-initiated studies. The institute also provides information and referrals on families and early childhood development and education. The organization's Web site features publications, announcements, and papers on early childhood development.

Parents Helping Parents

Sobrato Center for Nonprofits—San Jose
1400 Parkmoor Ave., Ste. 100
San Jose, CA 95126
(408) 727-5775
Web site: www.php.com

Parents Helping Parents (PHP) provides lifetime guidance, support, and services to families of children with any special need and the professionals who serve them. The organization's Web site provides contact information on resources available locally in cities throughout the United States.

U.S. Autism and Asperger Association

PO Box 532
Draper, UT 84020-0532
(801) 816-1234
Web site: www.usautism.org

U.S. Autism and Asperger Association (USAAA) is a nonprofit organization for autism and Asperger's education, support, and solutions. USAAA's goal is to provide the opportunity for individuals with autism spectrum disorders to achieve their fullest potential. The organization publishes a weekly newsletter, and the group's Web site has an extensive library on autism and Asperger's syndrome.

For Further Reading

Books

Ashley, Susan. *The ADD and ADHD Answer Book.* Naperville, IL: Sourcebooks, 2005. A reference book that provides advice and answers to many questions. The book includes questionnaires and checklists to help parents prior to their child's evaluation.

Barkley, Russell A., Kevin R. Murphy, and Mariellen Fischer. *ADHD in Adults: What the Science Says.* New York: Guilford, 2008. Provides a new perspective on ADHD in adults based upon two major studies directed by Barkley. Information is presented on the significant impairments produced by the disorder across major functional domains and life activities, including education, work, relationships, health behaviors, and mental health. Accessible tables, figures, and sidebars encapsulate the study results.

Bock, Kenneth. *Healing the New Childhood Epidemics: Autism, ADHD, Asthma, and Allergies.* New York: Ballantine, 2007. A clinician specializing in the biomedical approach to autism asserts that four common childhood disorders may share the same underlying causes, and offers a plan to reverse the symptoms of all four.

Buchman, Dana. *A Special Education: One Family's Journey Through the Maze of Learning Disabilities.* Cambridge, MA: Da Capo, 2006. Describes the story of the author and her daughter, Charlotte, who has learning disabilities. Buchman tells how she came to terms with her daughter's condition and the family's triumph over the daunting circumstances of learning disabilities.

Eide, Brock, and Fernette Eide. *The Mislabeled Child: How Understanding Your Child's Unique Learning Style Can Open the Door to Success.* New York: Hyperion, 2006. The Eides are a husband-wife team who run a neurolearning clinic in Washington State. Their book describes the brain processes that underlie different systems of learning of children who have been labeled autistic, ADHD, and the like, and offers steps that can be taken to help children whose processes fall into each category.

The Healing Project. *Voices of Autism: The Healing Companion: Stories for Courage, Comfort and Strength.* New York: La Chance, 2008. Relates real-life stories of lives transformed by autism. Perspectives include parents of autistic children and autistic adults living successfully. The book also contains a comprehensive resources section for those seeking help and information on the current state of autism research and treatment.

Heinkle-Wolfe, Peggy. *See Sam Run: A Mother's Story of Autism.* Denton, TX: University of North Texas Press, 2008. Relates the author's experience caring for her son, Sam, after he became uncommunicative and unmanageable. Her struggle to deal with her child's autism resulted in a transformation of her own ability to love and a new appreciation of her son.

Koegel, Lynn Kern, and Claire LaZebnik. *Growing Up on the Spectrum: A Guide to Life, Love and Learning for Teens and Young Adults with Autism and Asperger's.* New York: Viking, 2009. Describes interventions for managing life with autism, focusing on issues such as making and keeping friendships; dating, sex and romance; successful school experience; life beyond high school and college; and improving daily life. Each chapter features real-life narratives. The book demonstrates how kids with autism can function and thrive with dignity, self-respect, and autonomy.

McCarthy, Jenny. *Louder than Words: A Mother's Journey in Healing Autism.* New York: Dutton, 2007. Actress and TV personality Jenny McCarthy describes her life as the mother of an autistic child and what she has learned from the process.

Rosemond, John K., and Rose Bavenal. *Diseasing America's Children: Exposing the ADHD Fiasco and Empowering Parents to Take Back Control.* Nashville: Thomas Nelson, 2008. Argues that certain professionals and pharmaceutical companies have used faulty science to label millions of children with false illnesses. The authors assert that the science behind ADHD as it is currently defined is unraveling.

Whiffen, Leeann. *A Child's Journey Out of Autism: One Family's Story of Living in Hope and Finding a Cure.* Naperville, IL: Sourcebooks, 2009. A personal account of a young married couple's struggle after their child is diagnosed with autism.

Periodicals

Adams, Caralee. "Girls & ADHD: Are You Missing the Signs?" *Instructor (1990),* March 1, 2007.

Albemaz, Ami. "Smoking and Lead Exposure Could Contribute to ADHD," *Boston Globe,* September 25, 2006.

Altonn, Helen. "Hope for Autism Seen," *Honolulu Star-Bulletin,* April 12, 2008.

Baldauf, Sarah. "8 Questions Adolescents Are Asking About Stimulants: Addition Researchers Answer Teens' Questions about ADHD Medications," *U.S. News & World Report,* April 21, 2008.

Benson, Cathy. "Caring for Children with Autism," *Roanoke Times & World News,* March 28, 2008.

Burrell, Jackie. "Thriving with ADHD," *Oakland Tribune,* February 18, 2008

Cannell, John J. "Autism and Vitamin D," *Townsend Letter,* April 1, 2008.

Chang, Alicia. "Autism Cases Rise Despite Vaccine Ingredient Removal," *Deseret News* (Salt Lake City), January 8, 2008.

Conan, Neal. "Analysis: Adults with Learning Disabilities," *Talk of the Nation* (NPR), June 8, 2005.

Feldner, Claudia. "People with Learning Disabilities as Consumer Researchers," *Learning Disability Today,* May 1, 2007.

Foley, Nancy E. "Preparing for College: Improving the Odds for Students with Learning Disabilities," *College Student Journal,* September 1, 2006.

Goldberg, Carey. "Rare Genetic Hot Spot Is Linked to Autism," *Boston Globe,* January 10, 2008.

Gwynn, Hilary. "Learning Disabilities: The Pediatrician's Role," *Pediatric News,* April 1, 2008.

Hadley, Wanda M. "The Necessity of Academic Accommodations for First-Year College Students with Learning Disabilities," *Journal of College Admission,* April 1, 2007.

Jancin, Bruce. "Memory Training Lifts Some ADHD Symptoms," *Clinical Psychiatry News,* February 1, 2008.

Johnson, D. Richard, Daryl F. Mellard, and Paula Lancaster. "Road to Success: Helping Young Adults with Learning Disabilities Plan and Prepare for Employment," *Teaching Exceptional Children,* July 1, 2007.

Lovett, Benjamin J., and Lawrence J. Lewandowski. "Gifted Students with Learning Disabilities: Who Are They?" *Journal of Learning Disabilities,* November 1, 2006.

Lyon, Lindsay. "Treating ADHD Without Stimulants," *U.S. News & World Report,* April 21, 2008.

Mahoney, Diana. "Adults with ADHD Need to Know Treatment Options," *Clinical Psychiatry News,* September 1, 2007.

———. "Social and Emotional Costs of Learning Disabilities," *Clinical Psychiatry News,* February 1, 2008.

Neufeld, Paul, and Seanna Takacs. "Learning Disabilities, Schools, and Neurological Dysfunction," *Journal of Thought,* December 22, 2006.

Prater, Mary Anne, Tina Taylor Dyches, and Marissa Johnstun. "Teaching Students About Learning Disabilities Through Children's Literature," *Intervention in School & Clinic,* September 1, 2006.

Stein, Martin T. "Go with Experience for ADHD," *Family Practice News,* March 15, 2007.

Stolzer, J.M. "The ADHD Epidemic in America," *Ethical Human Psychology and Psychiatry,* January 1, 2007.

Vogel, Gila, Barbara Fresko, and Cheruta Wertheim. "Peer Tutoring for College Students with Learning Disabilities: Perceptions of Tutors and Tutees," *Journal of Learning Disabilities,* November 1, 2007.

Wright, Patricia. "Help and Hope for Families Living with Autism," *Exceptional Parent,* April 1, 2008.

Web Sites

Child Development Institute (www.childdevelopmentinfo.com/index .htm). Includes information on various disabilities affecting learning, offering articles on diagnosis, treatment, medication, and strategies for coping.

Mayo Clinic (www.mayoclinic.com/). Provides overviews and related articles on numerous disabilities affecting learning, including dyslexia, ADHD, and autism.

National Institute of Neurological Disorders and Stroke (www.ninds .nih.gov/disorders/autism/detail_autism.htm). Provides information about signs, diagnosis, and treatment of autism. The site also includes information about the role heredity may play in autism and offers an excellent list of related organizations.

National Institutes of Health (www.nimh.nih.gov/health/publications). Offers a wealth of information on autism and ADHD. Easy-to-read booklets on these topics are available for download. The site also includes scientific studies and the latest news about ADHD and autism.

Index

A

Abductions, 69

Abuse victims, children with learning
  disabilities as, 64–70

Adderall, *102*, 103

ADHD. *See* Attention deficit hyperactivity
  disorder (ADHD)

Adolescents
  adult expectations of, 60
  with behavior problems, 58–63
  employment preparation for, 121–125
  interventions for, 61–63
  risk-taking behavior by, 60

Adults, with ADHD, 24–28, 76–80, 111

Alcohol abuse, *59*

Ambidextrous, 8

Amphetamines
  calming effects of, 30–31, 101
  schools and, 35–36
  See also Ritalin

Amygdala, 72, *73*, *74*, 75

Anderson, Barbara, 97

Anti-psychotics, 108–109

Ascribe Higher Education News Service,
  81–85

Asperger, Hans, 9

Asperger's syndrome, 46, 47, 50, 53–54

Attention deficit hyperactivity disorder
  (ADHD)
  adults with, 24–28, 76–80, 111
  behavioral problems and, 62
  behavioral therapy for, 104–105
  characteristics of, 101
  controversy over, 9
  criteria for, 36, 37
  diagnosis of, 9, 36–37, 102
  educational attainment and, 26–27
  employment impact of, 27–28
  guidelines for treatment of, 113–114
  identification of, 8, 101
  impact of, on peer relationships, 81–85

income losses due to, 24–26, 77
  medications for, 32, 100–114
  misinformation about, 36
  as myth, 29–37
  overdiagnosis of, 103, 108–110
  overprescribed drugs for, 106–114
  problems caused by, 76–80
  rates of, 26
  as serious problem, 23–28
  treatment of, 9, 82–83
  types of, 8
  as typical childhood behavior, 33, 37
  worsening of, with drugs, 112

Autism
  age of diagnosis of, 39, 42
  brain changes and, 71–75
  causes of, 41–43, 48–49, 54–55
  classic, 53
  controversy over, 9
  as culturally acceptable, 47–48
  diversity in severity of, 51–55
  factors contributing to rise in diagnoses
    of, 44–50
  identification of, 9
  rates of, 39–41, 48–50
  research on, 49–50
  as serious problem, 38–43
  services for, 47–48
  symptoms of, 40–41, 45–46
  therapy for, 9
  treatment of, 48, 55

Autism Society of America, 9

Autism Speaks, 49–50

Autism spectrum disorders (ASD)
  criteria for, 9, 53
  diagnosis of, 46–47
  incidence rate of, 39
  medications for, 48
  range of, 52

Autistic children
  characteristics of, 45–46, 72–75

services for, 47
social interaction difficulties in, 40–41
as underserved, 40

B
Bates, Steve, 76–80
Baughman, Fred A., Jr., 29–37
Behavioral problems
  autism diagnosis and, 45–46
  drugging children with, 30–31, 35–36, 108
  explanations for, 34–35
  learning disabilities as cause of, 57–63
  reading difficulties and, 14–15
Behavioral therapy, for ADHD, 104–105
Benzedrine, 30, 31
Berlin, Rudolf, 7
Biederman, Joseph, 24, 26–27, 78–80
Bleuler, Eugen, 9
Boys, autism rates in, 41
Bradley, Charles, 30, 31, 101
Bradley, Emma Pendleton, 30
Bradshaw, Jim, 48
Brain, changes in linked to autism, 71–75
Brain function, 7
Brain injuries, 7, 32–33
Brazelton Neonatal Behavioral Assessment, 118
Briggs, Freda, 64–70
Brominated flame retardants (PBDEs), 119
Bullying, 69
Buxton, Craig, 112

C
"Capturing America's Attention" survey, 24–27
Carey, William, 36–37
Centers for Disease Control and Prevention (CDC), 39, 47
Chambers, Ellen, 95–96
Childhood behavior
  ADHD as typical, 33, 37
  tolerance for normal, 35
Children
  with ADHD, 81–85
  autistic, 40–41, 45–47, 72–75

drugging of unruly, 30–31, 35–36, 108
effects of toxin exposure in, 116–120
lead concentrations in, 117, 118
minority, 14–15
susceptibility of, to toxins, 116
Children with learning disabilities
  behavior problems in, 57–63
  employment preparation for, 121–125
  interventions for, 61–63
  isolation experienced by, 7, 9
  in schools, 96
  social skills instruction for, 125
  special education helps, 87–92
  vulnerability of, to abuse, 64–70
Chronic stress, 75
Ciba, 31
Citizens for Limited Taxation, 97
Clarkson, Amanda, 113
Coal-fired plant emissions, 118
Cocaine abuse, 111
Concerta, 112
Coping with Children's Temperament
  (Carey and McDevitt), 36–37
The Creation of Psychopharmacology
  (Healy), 31

D
Dalton, Kim, 74
Davidson, Richard, 72–74
Davis, Perry, 96
Deaths, from Ritalin, 108
Dees, Blake, 45–46
DeGrandpre, Richard, 103
Developmental disabilities, 117
Dexedrine, 31
Dextro-amphetamine, 31, 102
Diagnosis
  of ADHD, 9, 36–37
  of autism, 39, 42, 44–50
Diagnostic and Statistical Manual (DSM III), 8
Dopamine, 107
Douglas, Vivian, 8
Drug abuse, 69
Drug companies. *See* Pharmaceutical
  companies
Drugs. *See* Medications

Dyslexia
 defining, 19–22
 detection of, 13–14
 early intervention for, 13–14
 identification of, 7–8
 misunderstandings about, 17–22
 multisensory approach for, 14
 as myth, 18
 phonological deficit and, 12–13
 prevalence of, 12, 15, 19
 research on, 8
 as serious problem, 11–16
 teaching methods for, 8
 undiagnosed, 12
Dyslexic students
 intelligence of, 13
 neglect of, 12

E
Eddy, Barbara, *25*
Education. *See* Special education
Education of All Handicapped Children
 Act, 96
Educational attainment, ADHD and,
 26–27
Eisenberg, Leon, 31
Eli Lilly, 114
Emery, Chris, 38–43
Employment
 ADHD and problems with, 27–28,
  77–80
 preparation of learning-disabled
  students for, 121–125
Environmental factors
 in autism, 48–49
 in learning disabilities, 115–120
Expressive language disorders, 7
Eye contact avoidance, 73–74

F
Facial expressions, inability to identify,
 74–75
Fernard, Grace, 8
Fletcher, Daniel, 107
Fletcher, Hayley, 107, 111–112
Friendships, difficulties with, and ADHD,
 81–85

G
Gall, Franz J., 7
Gerberding, Julie L., 39
Gervais, Suzanne, 99
Gillingham, Anna, 8
Gladwell, Malcolm, 105
Goldstein, Gary, 39–43, 49–50
Growth stunting, 111

H
Hartman, Benjamin, 40–41
Hartman, Elisa, 40–41
Healy, David, 31, 36, 108–109, 111
Heavy metals, 118
Henry, Marynell, 94
Higgs, Steven, 40
High school dropouts, 58
Hinshelwood, James, 8
Hovey, Craig, 29–37
Hyperactive child syndrome, 8
Hyperkinetic reaction, 33

I
Immunizations, 41, 48–49, 54–55
Inclusion, 98
Income loss, from ADHD, 24–26, 77
Individuals with Disabilities Education
 Act (IDEA), 122
Interactive Autism Network, 49
Isolation, 7, 9

J
Janssen-Cilag, 114
Johnson, Richard, 121–125

K
Kanner, Leo, 9
Kendall, Tim, 109–110, 114
Kennedy, Edward, 96
Kennedy Krieger Institute, 39, 49
Kinesthetic learning strategies, 8
Kouris, Steven, 115–120
Kussmaul, Adolph, 7–8

L
Lancaster, Paula, 121–125
Language instruction, multisensory
 approach for, 14

Lead, 117, 118
Learning disabilities
  as cause of behavioral problems, 57–63
  prevalence of, 12, 58
  research on, 7–9
  special education to address, 87–92
  toxin exposure and, 115–120
  See also Children with learning
    disabilities
Lenane, Kevin, 98

M
Mahoney, Diana, 57–63
Mainstreaming, 98
Mann, Jennifer, 93–99
Massey, Chuck, 50
Massey, Julia, 50
Massey, Morgan, 50
Massey, Ryan, 45, 50
Massey, Trevor, 50
McDevitt, Sean, 36–37
McNamara, John, 60, 61
Medications
  for ADHD, 32, 100–114
  alternatives to, 113
  for autism spectrum disorders, 48, 55
  excessive dosages of, 111–112
  overprescribed, 106–114
  pushing of, by drug companies, 111
  side effects from, 103, 107–108,
    110–112
Mellard, Daryl F., 121–125
Mental retardation, 47, 48
Mercury, 41, 55, 118
Methylphenidate, 31, 102, 107
  See also Ritalin
Mikami, Amori Yee, 82–85
Mills, David, 17–22
Minimal brain dysfunction (MBD), 8,
  31–33
Minority children, 14–15
Mooney, Jonathan, 7
Multisensory teaching, 8, 14

N
National Institute for Health and Clinical
  Excellence, 114
National Institutes for Health, 71–75
National Longitudinal Study of
  Adolescent Health, 58
National Longitudinal Transition Study 2
  (NLTS-2), 123
National Survey of Children's Health, 58
Neeleman, David, 35
No Child Left Behind Act, 97
Nohle, Robert, 51–55
Novartis, 31, 114

O
Orfalea, Paul, 35
Organophosphate pesticides, 119–120
Orton, Samuel, 8
Orton-Gillingham teaching method, 8
Osher, David, 60–63

P
Parents
  blame of, for autism, 47
  of children with ADHD, 84–85
  misinformation about ADHD and, 36
Peer relationships, difficulties with, and
  ADHD, 81–85
Pelham, William, 111
Pervasive developmental disorder—not
  otherwise specified (PDD-NOS), 46,
  47, 53
Pesticides, 119–120
Pharmaceutical companies, 35–36, 111,
  114
Phonological deficit, 12–13
Polychlorinated biphenyls (PCBs), 118–
  119
Pornography, 66, 69
Porter, John W., 87–92
PR Newswire, 23–28
Pregnancy, toxin exposure in, 116
Psychiatry, 34–35
Public schools. *See* Schools

R
Reading
  components of, 13
  difficulties in, and behavior problems,
    14–15

as gift, 15–16
importance of, 12
Reading difficulties. *See* Dyslexia
Rice, Catherine, 39
Risk-taking behavior, 60
Risperdal, 107–112, 114
Ritalin
    effects of, 31–32
    increase in use of, 104, 113
    ineffectiveness of, 107
    lack of long-term benefits of, 110–111
    as overprescribed, *34*, 108–110
    prescriptions for, 103
    promotion of, 35–36
    response to, 102
    safety of, 114
    side effects from, 107–108, 111
    study of, 33

S
Sanghavi, Darshak, 100–105
Scheuplein, Eddie, 45
Schools
    autistic children as underserved in, 40
    behavioral problems and, 61–62
    bullying in, 69
    as drug pushers, 35–36
    employment preparation in, 121–125
    financial burden of special education
      on, 96
    number of learning disabled students
      in, 96
    resistance by, to special education, 90
Scott, Tom, 94
Sexual abuse, of children with learning
    disabilities, 65–70
Shepherd, Linda, 110
Shire Pharmaceuticals Group, 23
Silverman, Ralph, 97
Social fear, 72–73
Social interaction, difficulties with, 40–41
Social isolation, 7, 9
Social skills instruction, 125
Special education
    funding of, 90–92, 96–97

helps students with learning disabilities,
    87–92
inclusion and, 98–99
ineffectiveness of, 95–96
vs. regular education, 94–95
school resistance to, 90
spending on, 94–97
as too costly, 93–99
unequal services in, 90–91
SpEdWatch, 95–96
Speech and language therapy, 49
Speed. *See* Amphetamines
Spitzer, Robert, 101
Still, George, 8, 32
Stimulants
    calming effects of, 30–31
    market for, 35–36
    See also Ritalin
Stobbe, Mike, 44–50
Stotzner, Heinrich, 7
Stress, 75
Substance abuse, 69

T
Thimerosal, 49
Toxin exposure, 115–120
Treatment
    of ADHD, 9, 82–83
    of autism, 55
    See also Medications
Trevathan, Edwin, 47
Tyson, John, 112–113

V
Vaccinations, 41, 48–49, 54–55
Violence, against children with learning
    disabilities, 64–70

W
Wesby, E. Ruth, 11–16
Word blindness, 7–8
Workers with disabilities, 122–125

Z
Zyprexa, 107, 112, 114

Picture Credits

Maury Aaseng, 15, 19, 26, 32, 41, 49, 52, 62, 66, 74, 78, 84, 91, 95, 104, 113, 117, 124
AP Images, 25, 98, 109, 119, 123
© Roger Bamber/Alamy, 68
© Bubbles Photolibrary/Alamy, 10
© Jeff Greenberg/Alamy, 79
© Christina Kennedy/Alamy, 13
Will & Deni McIntyre/Photo Researchers, Inc., 46
© Brian Mitchell/Alamy, 42
© Max Palmer/Alamy, 59
Phanie/Photo Researchers, Inc., 54, 83, 88
© Phototake, Inc./Alamy, 34
Publiphoto/Photo Researchers, Inc., 86
JB Reed/Bloomberg News/Landov, 102
© vario images GmbH & Co.KG/Alamy, 21
WDCN/Univ. College London/Photo Researchers, Inc., 73
© Janine Wiedel Photolibrary/Alamy, 56